Praise for *Is This Seat Taken?*

"No matter how much we plan as individuals or as a company, the random encounter offers unplanned opportunity. Our files are filled with letters from customers who grasped the opportunity to take an empty seat next to their future soul mate during our flights. Kristin Kaufman will have you looking at chance encounters with a different perspective after reading this book."

—Gary Kelly
CEO, president, and chairman, Southwest Airlines

"Through real-life stories, Kristin Kaufman illustrates the core idea of being present in the moment and opening oneself up to new ideas in order to become an authentic leader in life."

—Stephen R. Covey
Author, *The 7 Habits of Highly Effective People* and *The Leader in Me*

"An inspiring and practical leadership handbook. Through powerful personal stories and great teaching points, Kristin challenges us all to be better leaders."

—Noel Tichy
Professor and director, Global Citizenship Initiative at the University of Michigan
Coauthor, *JUDGMENT: How Winning Leaders Make Great Calls* with Warren Bennis

"Kaufman has an uncanny ability to connect the wisdom of cab drivers and bartenders with the core issues of our everyday lives. Her colorful insights bring a smile—and often a laugh—of recognition in us all. If you are not lucky enough to share a cab or a glass of wine with Kristin, you can at least do one thing: read this book!"

—Robert W. Jordan
Former US ambassador to Saudi Arabia
Partner, Baker Botts, LLP

"I have always believed that you can learn something from every person who comes into your life. That's why I'm happy to recommend *Is This Seat Taken?* This collection of Kristin's 'chance' encounters may cause you to look at life—and every stranger you meet—a little differently. Read this book and take its lessons to heart."

—Ken Blanchard
Coauthor, *The One Minute Manager®* and *Lead with LUV*

"Cleverly written, *Is This Seat Taken?* delivers a powerful message through a series of eye-opening aha moments, with a sense of humor that will leave readers thinking long after the last page has been read."

—Bill Russell
Corporate executive, Hewlett-Packard

"A heartwarming book of chance encounters that points you toward how to align with your own deepest purpose. An inspirational read interspersed with meaningful personal reflections."

—**Barbara Braham**, PhD, MCC
Author, *Finding Your Purpose*

"As a global leader, Kristin Kaufman's perspectives in *Is This Seat Taken?* resonated with me and forced me to rethink incidental meetings that happen every day. Her concept of how these individuals can spark insights about our own alignment is thought-provoking and seminal for leaders. You can go as deep as you'd like or not—yet it is a journey worth taking."

—**Thomas E. Hogan**
Former executive vice president, Hewlett-Packard
CEO, Vignette Corporation

"A beautiful and joyous book on many levels, Kristin's stories showcase spontaneous examples of 'centered presence' in action. A 'sense of place' grounds many of these stories, as well as Kristin's curiosity and ability to engage others in the details of their lives. The stories have a transcendent quality yet a simple message: pay attention and get engaged in life. The stories remind us of the sacred, amazing life that is available to us. *Is This Seat Taken?* challenges us to remember what matters and brings inspiration to reconnect deeply to the moments each day brings to us."

—**Christine M. Wahl**, MAEd, MCC
Creator of the leadership coaching certificate program at Georgetown University
Faculty member, Georgetown University and George Mason University
Author, *Be Your Own Coach* and *On Becoming a Leadership Coach*

"Through her deep, intuitive understanding and unique way of building trust, Kristin has an extraordinary gift to collect and communicate stories that both teach and inspire us all!"

—**Wendy S. Lea**
CEO, Get Satisfaction

"The space between traditional business books and nonfiction memoirs offers some of the most thoughtful, authentic, and perspective-changing writing being done today. Kristin Kaufman's new book, *Is This Seat Taken?* is a welcome addition to that undefinable, yet most valuable, genre."

—**Jack Covert**
President and founder, 800CEOREAD

"*Is This Seat Taken?* offers simple, compelling lessons that change the way we see relationships and do business. Kristin Kaufman is brilliant in illustrating how chance encounters in our daily lives can provide rich opportunities to learn. I'll never take a conversation for granted again, whether with the person sitting next to me on the plane or the guy delivering my pizza."

—**Ann V. Deaton**, PhD, PCC
Managing partner, Bounce

Is This Seat Taken?

Taken?

Random Encounters
That Change Your Life

Kristin S. Kaufman

Brown Books Publishing Group
Dallas, Texas

Is This Seat Taken?
Random Encounters That Change Your Life

Brown Books Publishing Group
16250 Knoll Trail, Suite 205
Dallas, Texas 75248
www.brownbooks.com
(972) 381-0009

ISBN 978-1-61254-020-7
Library of Congress Control Number 2011935434

Printed in the United States of America
10 9 8 7 6 5 4 3 2 1

For more information, please visit www.KristinKaufman.com.

For my parents, the greatest blessings in my life

Table of Contents

Acknowledgments

I am grateful for the presence of a rich, wide, and diverse circle of friends, colleagues, and clients in my life and for the impact they have on my growth and ongoing development as a person. For the many who have shared this particular journey with me, and you know who you are, my sincere gratitude for your patience, interest, and encouragement through this process. Your generosity of time and spirit is realized and greatly appreciated.

My treasured sister, Gretchen, offered sisterly support throughout the entire process. She continued to paint the beautiful vision of where I had said I wanted to go and never for a moment questioned my ability to get there. Everyone should be so fortunate to have a sister as a life partner who challenges, questions, pushes, supports, and loves through life's learning experiences. I am a better human being because of my sister; and I am blessed beyond measure with this gift.

Most importantly, I want to express my extreme gratitude to my beloved parents. You trusted and believed in me from the beginning and never lost faith that my dream of writing this book could become a reality. Thank you for being the sole sets of eyes to read many of the initial stories and for giving me constant encouragement to follow my heart. Thank you for creating our family foundation of love, for raising and instilling in us the anchor of faith on which our lives are steadied, for the push and pull with which you challenged and encouraged us, for the love in which you enveloped us, and for the legacy you have provided us through your character, values, and life's example. You are the greatest blessings in my life, and for this alone, my cup runneth over.

Finally, this book would simply not have come to fruition without the support, encouragement, and guidance of a few seasoned talents in their fields. Ann Deaton, PhD, was a tremendous source of encouragement, unwavering confidence, and loyal friendship from the onset of this particularly journey. Thank you to Janet Harris and Ann Harper of Brown Books Publishing Group, who are amazingly gifted editors. When people declare they wish to write a book, I wonder if they fully realize what it takes emotionally and financially, not to mention the tremendous time commitment. Ann and Janet brought an exceptional wealth of wisdom, experience, and compassion to our writing partnership. The collective teams of Brown Books Publishing Group, Brooks & Associates Public Relations, and QuickSilver Interactive Group have been experienced shepherds from initial concept to creation, packaging, distribution, and ongoing delivery. I am grateful to have undertaken this project with a team of such devoted professionals. Writing can be a lonely endeavor; yet solitary work cannot be done alone. These professionals helped anchor my intention for my first book and accompanied me along this path with unwavering solidarity.

Author's Note

Most of us are on a quest to uncover what we really want to do with our lives, how we wish to contribute to the world, and what we want to do with the time we have on this planet. Given our innate uniqueness, our journeys will be different. Ideally our individual lives become perfectly integrated between what we love to do, what we are good at doing, and what gives us our greatest fulfillment. In other words—we are *aligned.*

My adulthood journey and professional career had been centered primarily in the corporate arena. Until a few years ago, my life had been a series of accomplishments, achievements, awards, and rewards. I experienced success on pretty much every level. Then I made the choice to "jump off the hamster wheel," listen and heed the whispers, and devote my energies to becoming truly integrated and "aligned" to my purpose. How did I come to this life-changing decision? Choices can and will almost always lead to change, and change definitely can be scary. Fear is the common paralyzer, and it nearly stopped me. Jumping was a sheer act of courage anchored in faith.

Along my journey of gaining greater self-awareness and ultimately embracing my true calling, I realized two important insights that helped me learn, grow, transcend, and include all parts of who I am. First, our greatest realizations happen when we live in the present moment. All we have is right now, this very moment. I have always been taught to "listen to the whispers" and our "inner voices," which we hear only when we are truly present. The whispers represent the choices that are within our reach. Frankly, I had certainly heard them over the years. I had just opted to ignore them. I didn't trust them. I allowed the intoxication of corporate life and all its trappings to shut out the messages. What I can say now is that through listening to my inner voice and trusting it, I opened my eyes to choices I did not truly realize I had.

The second realization, which took on new meaning for me, is that we are all part of an integral and collective experience in life. There are thousands of individuals who unknowingly help to create our life's journeys. These incidental players on life's stage often teach without deliberate intention. They teach through their simple actions, behaviors, and authentic presence. They teach through simply living their lives. The only requirement to benefit from their lessons and wisdom is to be present in the moment.

Each chapter in this book shares a vignette of one such incidental meeting and what I was reminded of through this serendipitous relationship. I also offer a few provocative questions for you to consider along your own journey. My intention in writing this book is to share a few of these experiences and how these seemingly unlikely individuals offered lessons that have served as guideposts along my personal road to alignment.

Life's journey is a miracle on many levels. It is enriched by the complexities of life and people. Our level of effectiveness, contribution, and integrity of work and life are in direct correlation with our level of integration, self-actualization, and total alignment of body, mind, and spirit. As I have come to appreciate, alignment begins with a constituency of one. These are the individuals whose substance is real, pure, and non-negotiable. They share their vulnerabilities and fears in complement to their strengths. They are comfortable weaving all parts of their lives together in an integrated way. I also have come to appreciate that alignment is the true differentiator of collections of individuals and successful organizations. I believe the most successful leaders are those who are congruent and fully aligned within themselves, to their organization, and ultimately to the customers and markets they serve. When this alignment is multiplied throughout an organization, the power is undeniable.

The answers are within us and are often revealed and amplified through unexpected interactions with others. By being awake and present in the moment, we allow our authenticity and ability to become fully aligned so this purpose can be revealed.

To See a World in a Grain of Sand
And Heaven in a Wildflower
Hold infinity in the palm of your hand
And Eternity in an Hour.
—William Blake

Wisdom
from a Cabbie

Steam bubbled up through the manholes like foam from a pot of boiling rice. In New York in July, stepping outside was like entering a sauna fully clothed and praying for a breath of wind. I was determined not to wilt before my first meeting.

"Park and Sixty-Fifth, please. And could we please roll up the windows and have some AC? Thanks."

Begrudgingly, the cabbie closed all the windows but his and turned the AC on low. I felt like a bug caught in a jar, confined in a hot sticky container with a few holes for air.

"Do you think we could turn the air up just a little? It is really hot back here."

A big sigh came from the front seat. "This eats my gas. No run AC. Better business."

"Thank you so much. I will make this worth your while, I promise. I just need to stay as cool as possible before my meeting. Just for a few blocks."

I realized I was living up to the spoiled white American woman stereotype in word and deed, but this man clearly was not trying to befriend me. He was providing a service for me—to cart me from point A to point B. Still, the people-pleasing side of me didn't want him to think ill of me. I wanted to win him over, so I began to focus on my taxi driver, pushing thoughts of my meeting aside for a bit.

"Polish or Russian?"

"Ukrainian," he answered gruffly and then added in heavily accented English, "How did you know so close?"

"I grew up with a man from Poland, and I recognized the . . . I am not sure what, frankly. How long have you been in New York?"

"Thirty years. Came here to get job. Good work here. More money."

"Is your family here?"

I was not sure if I was annoying him or if he was enjoying this banter. He looked into the rear view mirror and saw me looking back at him inquisitively. A looming figure, he gripped the wheel with hands so large they resembled calloused gloves.

"No. They still there. Came alone to get work."

"That must have been difficult. Did you speak English?"

"No. I learn. I listen and speak over the years. Drive taxi. Good money. Found wife—have two kids—married twenty-nine years. Good life. Happy. Good life."

"Do you ever visit your family? What do they do in Ukraine?"

"Yes. I get to see them every three or four years. I go home. They have acre of land. They grow vegetables for village. They are still there. Very old, now."

"Will you ever move back?"

"Oh, no. Very poor country. They work and work—never get ahead. Much drink over there. Life hard. Here you have chance.

Here you have work and have house. I am US citizen. Took test. Not good English—yet believe in America."

"You left your family to come over here by yourself to get a job over thirty years ago? Do you mind if I ask how old you are?"

He laughed playfully, "Oh, no. I am forty-eight years."

I nearly lost any decorum my mother had taught me about polite conversation. This man looked to be at least seventy years old. His face was as creased and dark as the tires on his taxi. The circles under his eyes were deep and murky.

"You are young! You have your entire life ahead of you. And your children? How old are they?"

"They twenty-eight and twenty-nine. Girl and boy. Both married. They work hard. Have three grandchildren in school. Hope to get good education. Good jobs."

We neared my destination, but before I got out, I had two more questions. "What led you to where you are today? Is anything missing for you?"

He answered calmly, "I wanted more. I wanted to be more than a vegetable grower. I wanted to work for myself, not others. I long for nothing. I have job. We are blessed. We have love. We have family. We have freedom." He smiled a crooked grin.

As I dug through my purse trying to find the ever-elusive coin purse, I thought, *I set out to win him over, and what really happened was just the opposite.* I handed him a handsome tip—not for the AC, for the life's lesson on what the manifestation of courage looks like.

The Courage to Take the First Step

As I thought back on this unexpected interaction, one thing kept entering my mind: *this man was so brave*! He embarked on a journey no one in his family, much less his village, had ever taken, and at a time when the Internet and other supporting resources were not readily available. He powered through his fears, and this quality of unbridled bravery set his life on a course that altered his destiny. Fortunately I had put aside fretting over my meeting and focused on the human being with whom I shared these few minutes, and I was the one rewarded with a "tip."

This driver knew who he wanted to be! As he reached adulthood, he must have realized his success was to be created in the United States. He began to align his goals powered by the courage he mined deeply from within to achieve his dream. Overcoming obstacles, unprecedented creativity, and unwavering solidarity contributed to creating his life. I find it hard to grasp fully the effort this man exerted to get there. By being present to the moment, I was given this gift of meeting raw courage face-to-face.

Being aligned and ultimately fulfilled in business and life requires courage and perseverance. How do we muster the courage to heed our inner voice when it may require us to swim against the current? How can we develop the fortitude to stand tall in the face of adversity? How can we align our goals and dreams with enough courage to achieve them? What this experience revealed to me is that when we proclaim our fearlessness, we can become fearless. This is a choice. It will not happen "to" us; we make a decision to be brave, to look fear in the face, and assume the position. This Ukrainian cab driver certainly must have been afraid, leaving all he ever knew to pursue a dream in a country he had never even seen and of which he did not even speak the language. Yet he chose to come here anyway and persevered.

Recently I worked with an executive who needed to give a very public report on the company's less-than-glowing quarterly results. The recession had impacted his business, and there was a simple "lack of execution" against defined objectives. The report he would present would be negative, and the audience, made up of analysts and shareholders, would cut him no slack. He was scared.

Nevertheless he needed to stand up, tell the truth, and lay out his next course of action. He had to get past his fear. Every morning as he was shaving, he recited a mantra to himself: "I am strong. I can do this. We will be successful going forward. I am not afraid." Before long, he began to embody those very words. Giving his quarterly analysis report was tough, yet he demonstrated strength, confidence, and courage when he stood before a very demanding audience. *He assumed the position.*

Just like the taxi driver, this executive made a choice to persevere. Courage and perseverance are integral to our quest for alignment in business and in life. Courage is embraced when we dare to follow our inner voice, instincts, and intuition even when outside voices and pressures may encourage another direction. Courage may be seen when we take a loyal stand opposing a group of friends when they betray or choose to exclude another friend. We may witness it when a corporate board executive passionately presents an alternative strategic direction for the company that opposes the collective opinion of the rest of the board. Courage may be seen when a "whistle blower" refuses to lie through either blatant commission or subtle omission while being publicly questioned about a corporate accounting misrepresentation. And certainly, courage and persistence are keys to navigate and power through seemingly impossible obstacles on our life's journeys.

In our daily lives, whether leading in corporate America, teaching school, raising teenagers, or driving a cab, we are often faced with the temptation to cower or "give up" when life's tests get tough. If we give in to our fears in any position in life, we truncate our individual potential and our personal and professional opportunities. This Ukrainian taxi driver reminded me that the first step to creating alignment of our hopes, dreams, and goals is having the sheer courage to pursue them. In my life, this meant "jumping off the high board," leaving what was familiar and safe to explore and ultimately create what I really wanted. As individuals and leaders, in whatever capacity—parents, teachers, corporate executives, school principals, entrepreneurs, and friends—we have a responsibility to be courageous and persevere in the face of often scary, ominous, and risky circumstances. We never know who may be looking to us for our resolve, our clarity of direction, our stalwart example, and our persistent *courage* to make the hard decisions, to stand tall against opposing currents, and to stay true always to our convictions.

Examples of courage are all around us if we take a moment to listen and experience life through another individual's courageous journey. If we are fortunate, we might even become someone's incidental encounter that influences that person to be present in the moment and courageously move toward alignment.

Being Present in the Moment:
Moving Toward Alignment

Questions to consider:

- What behaviors and thought patterns help you overcome fear? Can you envision a previous triumph? What can you learn from your success in that particular situation?
- What do you want to pursue, but you are afraid to take the plunge? What is holding you back?
- Have you ever been an "incidental" person in someone else's life? Do you recognize even the initial impact you might make in a brief encounter?

Man cannot discover new oceans unless he has
the courage to lose sight of the shore.
—Andre Gide

A
Moment's
Connection

The rancid stench of curry, sweat, and ashy smoke created air as heavy as concrete, nearly impossible to breathe without some sort of filter. The colorful saris being dipped in the Ganges River for cleansing and purification in the putrid water were equally as penetrating to the senses. Even so, the morning was magical as I meandered down the filthy pathway with curbs formed of mud, trash, and rotten waste.

At 5:30 a.m. on the third day of what I fondly call one of my spiritual odysseys, I was on my way for a morning canoe cruise with my guide, Rajiv, to take in the sunrise on the Ganges. The sky in northern India was pitch-black with streaks of yellow just beginning to reach above the horizon like crooked, arthritic fingers. The morning dew cast a veil of gray gauze on the scene.

The name "Ganges" means much more than "flowing water"; for spiritual seekers, it represents life, purity, and a goddess to the people of India. The story of "Mother Ganges" is an incredible myth of how she poured herself down from heaven upon the ashes of King Sarga's sons. Her waters raised them to dwell in peace in heaven. Hindus believe that anyone who touches these purifying waters is cleansed of all sins. The Ganges is a place where life and death meet. It draws all kinds of people, and life seems to be continually bustling at its side.

That morning as we walked down the winding path, the world was just awakening to both lightness and darkness. The *ghats* were being readied for their final rituals. Washer women beat their clothes on stones at the edge. Multicolored saris and all sorts of wet clothes were laid out to dry in the sunshine. An enchanting tapestry of humanity congregated.

I thought my soul must be saturated with just about every emotion imaginable, and then I looked up from the muddy track I was forging. On a small platform no more than six by eight feet, elevated twelve or so feet off the ground by four spindly stilts, something or someone moved.

A single lightbulb suspended to a makeshift outlet like a giant paperclip was attached to the main electrical line for the street. The dim glow just barely illuminated the sparse perch. A man and a woman were lying on what looked like a mound of rags, just waking up and cooing to a small infant nestled between their two bodies. Their focus was on this child as they lay on the cloth-covered plank with only the back side of their makeshift home sheltered. I was touched and aghast. Amid such poverty and filth, I felt a strange sense of warmth.

"Rajiv, wait. Look."

"What? Why?"

I gestured with my eyes up to the waking family. "Oh, Rajiv. This is so terribly sad. Look where they live. Where do they eat? Where do they bathe? Is this really their home? They have a new baby, and they appear destitute."

"Kristin, you need not worry about this. They are happy. Look at them. They know nothing else. They don't miss what they have never had. They have new life between them. It is all good."

"But how? Look where they live. Look at the filth and poverty around them. What can be good about this?"

"Wealth is in the mind. Love is in the heart. All else reveals itself in time. Westerners have a hard time with this."

My mind knew what Rajiv had said was spiritually true, yet I felt strangely vacuous as if my life up to this point had suddenly been reduced to a small pellet. As we continued to make our way to the river bank, the smell of burning flesh grew even more potent, and we met the masses of color from the fray of beggars, worshipers, and the grieving. Rajiv and I joined our oarsman and coasted onto the Ganges just as the sun rose over the horizon. This tranquil though enigmatic moment was a paradox of riches, emptiness, and inconsolable compassion.

We were silent. There was no wind, as if the sky had sucked any extra breeze into its mouth. My skin became sticky with the summer humidity. The only sound we heard was the lazy lapping of the wake caused by the oarsman steering our course with his long wooden paddle. As I looked to the edge of the earth, the sun had now crawled up the dark night's blanket and cast a soft hazy hue of peach above the horizon. The reflection sparkled on the river's ripples, and this image transported me to another surreal sanctuary.

I began to create my own story of this glimpse into humanity, the couple with their newborn baby. Their love appeared pure and simplistic with no material hooks or requirements. Perhaps they truly were in bliss. Surrounded by squalor and living next door to an outdoor crematorium, they carved out their life with love.

As we neared the shore line, I saw a collection of lotus blossoms near the bank. In the eastern traditions and the myth of Indra, the lotus blossom is the symbol of the unification of earthly energy and divine grace.

"The Greatest of These . . ."

Life and death were indeed near on this bank in Varanisi. On this morning many years ago, by being present in that moment and peering through this small window of humankind, I recognized a fundamental truth. The sole self-awakening antidote to hopelessness is love. We all carry an image of our world in our heads, and often we are shocked when we come face-to-face with the realities of where and how this image may differ. Though their home was a mere plank with a solitary lightbulb, I chose to believe this couple had created a life bound by love.

I have no knowledge into their lives outside this seemingly utopic moment. What I do know is that love is the great unifier. Love exists, blossoms, and binds under any condition. Love smoothed the raw edges of their grim survival. Love is the light illuminating our way to alignment. This couple opened the door to a long hallway of growing awareness. I was reminded that we are here to learn and teach through love. On that day, I was the student.

Being Present in the Moment: Moving Toward Alignment

Questions to consider:

- What brought Rajiv to the point where he could gaze upon the desperately poor couple and their newborn with such compassionate understanding?
- What connection do you feel to this couple, though their circumstances are light-years away from yours?
- How does love permeate your life and smooth the rough edges?

And now these three remain: faith, hope, and love.
And the greatest of these is love.
—1 Corinthians 13:13

Just Lean On Me

The day was like any other—except I was being admitted into the hospital to have a surgery that would change my life forever. My mask of strength was frayed and a bit threadbare from the wear and tear of the prior ten months. The road traveled up to this point had been riddled with hairpin curves to arrive at the most recent diagnosis.

While I was being admitted into the hospital, the combination of alcohol infused with institutionally reincarnated air brought back memories of prior hospital stays. I went through the standard admission procedure, was prepped for surgery, and had an operation that held my future in a balance. Ultimately, despite the life-saving prognosis, I knew that losing the ability to have children was a unique grief that lasts a lifetime, understood only by those enduring it.

Awakened that afternoon by the pain, I found the morphine pump a welcome companion. With the DVT leg compression contraptions, I resembled an astronaut from the waist down. The multiple tubes from the waist up gave me a sense that, if I had been plugged into an electrical outlet, I could have wired NASA directly to launch me to the moon.

"Good morning, Kristin! My name is Mary. I'm going to be your nurse for the next shift. How're you feeling? Let's see, we need to get you some fresh ice chips." This was my first splash of Mary; I would be fully immersed in her kindness and strength before leaving the hospital.

"Can you please do something to help relieve this pain?"

"Oh, sweetie. I know it hurts. Now don't you be hesitant to push that little pump. You just keep on pushing away—you can't OD—and don't wait till it hurts. You need to keep that medicine in your system. Let's get you some fresh ice chips. How'd you like to have cold cloths around your neck and on your forehead?"

Before I could answer, Mary came back and gently washed my face, neck, hands, and forearms, carefully avoiding the numerous tubes. I felt cooler and, strangely, a slight bit better.

"I'll be back later. You just rest, and I'll see you in a little while."

In her late fifties, Mary had skin like chocolate chip ice cream, dark with dots of candy sprinkled on top. Her black hair was thick and full with a silvery gray hairline framing her face. Her bright smile was buoyed by a red pair of lopsided lips. She walked with a slight stoop forward, which made her bottom protrude like a punctuation point. She strode with conviction, as if she knew where she was going, tilted toward her next patient and ready to offer comfort.

As I lay there between drug-induced sleep and the constant interruptions of the nurse's aides taking my temperature and blood pressure, I wrestled with the possibility of having cancer, never having my own DNA family, and the raw resentment of helplessness. My childhood dreams were shattered. My prior expectation of life was truncated as abruptly as pinching off the heads of rosebuds.

"Good morning! How're you feeling?" Mary burst into the room like a ray of sun poking through a stormy sky. "I see you are off the drip. Good. Today we're going for a walk. Can you sit up for me?"

I reached for the suspended iron bar above my bed and gripped it like a trained Olympic athlete mastering a parallel routine. Slowly I pulled myself up, wincing from the pain.

"Good job. Can you swing your legs over to the side? I've got you. Just lean on me."

And with a motion that resembled an old Saint Bernard rolling over, I was sitting on the edge of the bed, feeling a bit lightheaded, yet steadied by the human steel standing by my side. As Mary propped me up, we began to shuffle across the room, the first steps in my journey back to health.

This became our daily dancing date. Each morning and afternoon, Mary would come to my room to help me hobble the halls of the hospital. She gave me sponge baths, brought ice chips and juice, and brushed my hair. When tubes needed to be added or removed, Mary was there. When visitors brought flowers or cards, Mary received them. When doctors visited to give updated reports, Mary was with me.

The day came for my bandages to be removed. Mary helped me out of the bed, and we slowly made our way to the bathroom where Mary had started a warm shower.

"You just sit right here and let the water run over these adhesives. There, there. Now . . ." Before I could say a word, Mary ripped the bandage off like an aesthetician waxing eyebrows. "Good girl—now doesn't that feel wonderful?"

I choked on my breath. As if a cork had been suddenly

removed, my emotions spilled everywhere, and my body shook uncontrollably.

"Oh, I'm so sorry. I didn't mean to hurt you," Mary soothed.

"No, no. It's not that," I whispered between sobs. "I am just sad. I am just so sad. It is so final."

And without even a hint of hesitation, Mary took possession like a lioness with her cub. After getting me warmly snuggled back into bed, she listened patiently and intently to the sorrow and sense of loss I shared. I whimpered as I talked of my disappointment, sense of finality, and newly revealed lack of clarity for my life's direction.

All this time, Mary just held my hand and stroked it as if she were petting a newborn puppy. Then she gently whispered, "You know, Kristin. Every minute and every event of our life imprints something on our soul. I honestly can't imagine losing the ability to conceive children, yet you're here for a unique purpose. Bearing your own children won't be part of your life, yet there will be other experiences unique for you. Trust in that. Choose that. Embrace that."

I was discharged from the hospital the following day. I went home with a void in my body, but I also remembered Mary's words and chose to consider my new future open to new and different opportunities. The surgery had changed my life forever, yet I hoped I would eventually embrace a different future direction for my life because of my gift from Mary.

When Life Changes Your Dreams

While I was in the hospital, I never saw or experienced anything but effervescent energy, can-do spirit, and clarity of purpose from Mary. When I left the hospital, I could have chosen to think of myself as empty and barren; instead, thanks in large part to Mary, I chose to consider my life and body as my vessel, ripe for new creativity and contribution. She healed, listened, and empowered. Mary was in love with her job. Her soul's purpose was in total alignment with her profession.

Alignment is powerful. Once individuals are truly aligned around their life's purpose, they are indeed living in fulfillment. I believe that the most successful individuals are those whose thoughts, feelings, beliefs, gifts, talents, strengths, preferences, and desires about how and where to contribute in the world are aligned. Their mind, body, emotions, and spirit are in harmony.

When we see a person who truly walks their talk, whose life is a full and total manifestation of their beliefs, and whose profession is one that fully capitalizes on and optimizes their gifts and talents, we see a person on the right path. We do not have to look too far for examples; aligned individuals would do their jobs for free and come to work with a spring in their steps. They are the ones who have a passion for their work, an intense desire to make a difference, and a sense of being centered and confident. Their personal and professional goals are aligned, and they find joy in fulfilling their purpose.

Mary is such a person. Her job is not an easy one; there is heavy lifting, literally and figuratively, in the ward where she works. Emotionally and physically, she witnesses pain, heartache, disappointment, and fear. Many of us would cower at the thought of serving humanity in this way, yet her calling is authentic. She is powerful. I came through my experience stronger because of Mary.

There are many public figures aligned with their unique purposes. Think of global figures who have made monumental life-changing contributions, such as Nelson Mandela, Ghandi, and Mother Teresa. Think of artists who have followed their dreams against many obstacles to give the world their creative genius, such as Itzhak Perlman, Leontyne Price, and Mikhail Baryshnikov. Their unique gifts and talents were aligned with their innermost desires and intentions, and the results were phenomenal.

How can we become more aligned? We must listen to our hearts by paying attention to that little voice inside. It may come as a question in the middle of the night, or it may be as crystal clear as a voice in the shower. That voice is our soul, our core, and the pure essence of what and who we are meant to be.

Mary instinctively knew what alignment meant for her, and her embracing that knowledge revealed her authenticity so that she could most passionately impact others' lives. Her power was not that of the business, political, or social world but of her congruency of mind, body, heart, and spirit. We can all learn from Mary a lesson about the secret to living our lives with powerful purpose and purposeful power.

Being Present in the Moment:
Moving Toward Alignment

Questions to consider:

- How have major losses in your life altered your focus for the future?
- What lessons can you learn from Mary and her approach to life? What choices are clearly being manifested in her life?
- What are the common characteristics of people who live in alignment?

Happiness is when what you think,
what you say, and what you do are in harmony.
—Mahatma Gandhi

Where Is There?

As she entered, her carriage spoke of a strident Upper East Side constraint punctuated by a Hollywood Boulevard swagger, commanding full attention from both genders. Her pink Chanel suit cupped her wiggly parts in a way that would embarrass women of an older generation. She had white-blonde hair and a face that wouldn't move even if Robin Williams gave his best comedic stage performance. The gift of Botox and a wind tunnel facelift left a perpetual look of awe and excitement painted on her face.

She was the stereotypical Barbie doll, perched on her Jimmie Choo stilettos, clasping her Louis Vuitton as if it were her passport to freedom. She slid onto the barstool in the exaggerated way which resembled everything about her, and then crossed her hourglass legs to make a perfect figure eight closed at the ankles.

"Hello, Fritz! How *are* you today? Ketel One martini, up, dry, with a twist. Thank you soooo much."

She lifted the martini to her lips as if it was rare nectar saved for the most special, exquisite occasions, making sure that her four carat, emerald-cut diamond caught the light. She left her fuchsia tattoo on the rim of the glass as she took a sip. She closed her eyes, savoring the moment.

An elderly gentleman sat sipping on a half-empty drink nearby. With his tortoise-shell reading glasses at the tip of his nose, he was perusing a small magazine. He had a regal bearing despite his rumpled dress. He glanced at Fritz, tipped his head denoting *another, please,* and then looked over at me.

"What are you having?" he asked in a deep British accent. "May I treat you to another?"

I was taken a bit off guard, as I was immersed in watching the antics of the blonde and the others also watching the antics of the blonde. "That is so nice of you. Thank you. I am having a glass of the Bordeaux."

"Fritz, another glass for the lady, please." He ordered with the confidence of both familiarity and experience. "Are you here on holiday or business?"

"Business. I actually arrived earlier this week, and my meetings finished today. I will be flying on to Paris early tomorrow."

That's how it started. Two strangers at a bar, striking up what typically begins as an idle exchange. Simon was his name. I learned he lived not far away, in a townhome in the Belgravia area of London. A widower with three sons and six grandchildren, he had been a successful business executive and had retired several years prior. He spent his time taking weekend trips to visit his grandchildren in the Cotswolds, keeping his mind active through managing his investments, and playing backgammon with his cronies. He came to this particular neighborhood bistro every Thursday to read and have a few single malt scotches in the company of Fritz and a few other regulars.

After we had bantered about all the obvious particulars of our respective lives, he said to me, "You see that woman over there?"

pointing with his eyes to the blonde at the bar. "Now, that's a story worth telling." I looked at him curiously. "She is here two or three times a week."

"By herself?" I asked.

"Sometimes a friend meets her here. She was married to a very successful man. Divorced now. You know, that lady always wanted more, more, more. My wife and I have known her since she was in her late twenties. Our oldest is about her age. She has always been driven for or to something. Always wanting to go 'somewhere' and become 'someone' other than who she is. If there were a royal event, society function, or charity effort, she simply had to be involved front and center."

He gazed into his scotch as if he studied the swirls long enough, they would provide the answer.

"My wife and I could never figure her out. Her first husband was a gem of a guy. They had two precious children, about the age of my two middle grandchildren. She had a wonderful life. Yet she was always climbing. She pushed and pushed. She was trying to get somewhere else, to get 'there,' and we could never figure out where 'there' was for her. Where did she think she was going? I can't help but wonder where she is now, really."

In the time "Blondie" took to order another martini, Simon and I had moved from fun cocktail chatter to the baring of souls. This was not something I expected from a seventy-plus-year-old Brit in a small neighborhood canteen. Perhaps the lubrication of scotch prompted Simon to open up so freely, but his compassion was undeniably genuine.

"Simon, what do you think drives her for more? She never had 'more' growing up? Is she constantly competing with others to be recognized? Must she be superior to feel whole? Does she need 'stuff' to make her feel worthy?"

"Those are the questions, aren't they? I can't answer them for her. I can answer only for me. Comparison is a game we will never win. I know that fulfillment comes from within, not from a higher rung on the corporate ladder, a larger portfolio, or higher social standing but from being the best 'me,' whatever that evolves to be, by and through my choices. There is real peace and contentment when I know that."

He watched the blonde for a moment as she posed and ordered another drink.

"I lost my wife too soon, but the life we had together was wonderful. We loved each other immensely. We were not the wealthiest by material standards. We were not the thinnest or youngest looking for our age, yet we were happy and joyful in our lives. I am convinced, looking back, that we always felt we had 'arrived' to use the term of today's generation. We believed we were already 'there.'"

Simon and I continued to enjoy a lovely evening together. As I left, "Blondie" was still at the bar. Perhaps she was indeed seeking something from the outside which was already inside, had she understood to look there. I will never know what happened to her or if she made peace with herself, but that experience so many years ago was a catalyst for my personal alignment journey.

Finding "There" . . . Here

What Simon shared with me so many years ago was infinitely wise. I believe he realized that the source of all abundance was within. He knew that all the answers reside within us. No person, societal declaration, or journalist defines who we are. No station in life, bank account, or *Fortune* ranking creates our meaning, declares our purpose, or defines our success.

In the *nouveau riche* western society, this insatiable desire of wanting "more" and arriving "somewhere" is commonplace. Our culture's center of gravity is all about achieving and wanting more and more. When do we know when we have "enough"? When is our thirst for "more" quenched? What drives people to have everything that others think they could ever want—and yet still want more?

Success is aligning who we really are inside our souls with what we do and how we contribute in the world. We manifest our purpose in our actions. Our jobs and positions may change— and probably will. These changes may come from encounters like the ones in this book, through a forced situation like being fired or relocated, or through an "epiphany" which we cannot explain except to say to ourselves, "I know this is what I need to do." When our internal desires, passions, and intentions align with how this manifests into the world *each moment,* "there" becomes "here."

When we are living each moment for the sheer joy of what that moment is, we are aligned. This may occur while selling a computer, teaching a student, running a company, or treating a patient. The fulfillment is not through the monetary reward or achievement of the task at hand. Fulfillment, success, and what many may call the "end game," is in the actual moment in which we find ourselves, not some future time or place. That is being in alignment in the present moment and through our authentic selves.

Many of us are seeking and striving to become "something" or "someone." We are striving to get "there." Where is *there*? We place this destination in the future, as if once we arrive, we will have everything that will make us happy. This destination is fictitious, for all we really we have is now, and all we need we already have within us. The irony is that there is no "there," as Gertrude Stein so wisely said. There is here.

Being Present in the Moment: Moving Toward Alignment

Questions to consider:

- Where is "there" by your definition?
- Are your values and goals congruent with your true self?
- If others close to you could assess your journey, would they say that your goals are aligned to your authentic self?

Now is the only time we have.
—Elisabeth Kubler-Ross

Bakti

At several thousand feet above ground, life seemed to slow to a surreal pace. As we flew over these sweeps of Himalayan grandeur, I felt as if I were being held in God's palm and these peaks were his fingers cradling me. I was lost in a trance when the captain came over the loudspeaker to tell us to get ready for landing.

Later when I came upon the Durbar Square, in the old city of Kathmandu, my eyes immediately locked on the oft photographed two-story pagoda, *Kasthamandap*. The centuries-old structure had been built from a single tree with no iron nails or supports.

As we strolled through the streets of this ethereal town, I sensed the history emanating throughout the city. The colorful flags hanging around every building flew wildly in the wind. The mystical *Puja* bells sang the Buddhist songs of life. Walking down the winding path, lined with the *Swayambhunath* prayer wheels and Buddhist monks silently meditating, I had a sense of sanctuary. I found myself walking almost reverently.

As I peeked into doorframes, I found peddlers selling everything from fresh lemons and limes to handwoven fabrics. In one alcove, I saw an old man sitting on the dirt floor next to a fire pit. Two black irons turned red hot from the coals. I watched as he picked up one of the irons with his foot, which was swathed in a layer of rags. His foot looked like a giant callus with bulbous marbles for toes. He began to iron what looked like a long robe on a flat wood plank, with a gymnast's ambidextrous maneuvers. Next to him was a small basket of coins, his daily collection of wages.

As my eyes made their way to his face, I saw a raisin looking back at me with black flea eyes. His expression was one of quiet resolve and disregard. I stood there lost in a moment of translucent mortality wondering how he thought of life or if he even did.

As I meandered through the town, I came upon a small courtyard. A trickling water hydrant attracted women with their buckets and urns, each waiting a turn while their children nearby made games with sticks, dirt, and air. As we intruded upon this daily ritual, the children took notice of the light-skinned, western-dressed visitors. Most of them skittishly ran to the security of their moms' skirts. All except one.

This little girl, no more than four or five years old, was looking at me with cautious curiosity in her spoon-size brown eyes. She timidly walked toward me holding her toy twig, never losing her gaze. She was dressed in a pale pink, frayed frock with faded flowers on it, which looked as if it had been worn by several older sisters before it had made its way to her. Her bare feet were caked in dust, and her knees were the color and texture of tree bark.

"Hi, my name is Kristin," I said quietly.

She quickly looked down coyly, blinked a few times, and then peered back. She walked closer and extended her toy twig to me like a gift. I smiled and thanked her by putting my hands together in a prayer gesture and then motioned for her to sit next to me on the stone wall nearby.

Because of the language barrier, I began to mime conversation with her. We drew cartoon caricatures of animals and flowers in the dusty dirt with her toy twig and quietly giggled. Her gentle spirit and childish view of her world were contagious. That little patch of earth became a canvas on which we created an imaginary world. Our visions were unified through playful expressions.

We played together for quite some time before her mother, laden with water-filled urns, came to collect her daughter. As she rose to meet her mother, I was wistful. For a brief moment, we had been lost in our own world, getting to know each other. The expression "pleasure through simple things" had a fresh meaning for me.

I wanted to give this little girl something as a parting gift. In my bag, I found a ballpoint pen and gave it to her with a small spiral notebook I used to capture key thoughts about places and things from my trip. I showed her how to push the top of the pen to make it write. Her eyes sang, and her smile exploded excitement. That joyous look on her face lingers with me still.

She looked up at her mother as if to say, "Do you see this? Can you see this? Mom, *look at this*!" Then she reached out and threw her arms around my neck and squeezed hard.

As I walked away to find my friends, that strange surreal feeling I had several thousand feet above the earth a few days earlier returned to me.

Connected Heart-to-Heart

Despite being surrounded by astounding temples and captivating smells, when I met this little cherub, I was completely drawn into her world. Seldom in my busy life do I find myself so intensely swallowed by the moment. Her innocent gratefulness and enthusiastic joy from a dirt canvas and twig paintbrush was humbling and touching. We entered her imaginary world and together created an entire universe from bits of ground. I wondered if she imagined the same dreams as little girls from my country.

Though we are different, we are the same. We make connections, friends, and relationships with others walking the same human journey. We learn and grow—some from formal study, others from apprenticing under a mentor, and all of us from life's experiences. This little girl would be almost twenty years of age now. I wonder where she lives, if she is married, if she has children of her own, and how she is contributing to the world. I want to believe her imagination is still free and untethered, and that she is bringing that same refreshing, resourceful perspective to life.

Kathmandu still remains one of my favorite places in the world but not solely for the mystical energy which enveloped me. My purest memory is my brief time with this little girl. Though no words were spoken, a sublimely rich experience and powerful connection were made through authentically sharing a simple experience. She was the gift Kathmandu gave me.

Being Present in the Moment: Moving Toward Alignment

Questions to consider:

- What seemingly insignificant moment have you let pass without recognizing what it might offer?
- How can adopting a childlike perspective of wonder and simplicity help solve problems, approach new experiences, and build thriving relationships?
- How can you revive the childlike sense of awe and joy in yourself, your friends and colleagues, and your life?

The silence often of pure innocence
persuades when speaking fails.
—William Shakespeare

Seat 5E

H eading home?" he asked with an energetic voice, way too lively for 8:30 on a Friday night.

I had worked up a clammy sweat rushing to the gate to catch my flight, dragging my luggage behind me. I was ready for something cold, preferably with spirits. I was busily compartmentalizing the week into nice, orderly mind files as I collapsed into my seat. I could hardly wait to disappear for a few hours into anonymity and read some trashy Hollywood magazine. I didn't want to think smart, act smart, or be smart.

I sighed, smiled, and said quietly, "Home." I retreated into my *People* magazine as if it were *Barron's Daily* and held the answer to the world's recessionary problems.

"That's always a nice feeling. Me, too. Can't wait to see my children. Tomorrow is Tommy's eighth birthday. We have an entire flight museum deal planned. You have kids?"

At this point, I knew the horse was out of the barn. I must have an invisible neon sign, flashing on my forehead, saying: "If you need someone to listen, sit by me!"

"No, no children. Just a four-legged niece." I focused my sights on the "best dressed list" with a deliberation even Vera Wang would have respected.

Thanks to the competing overhead announcements, our conversation was halted until after takeoff. We had been upgraded and were enjoying the warmed nuts and cocktails before our dinner service, but I suspected the brief reprieve was too good to last.

John began to tell me about his twenty-year career with a large *Fortune* 50 healthcare company. He had been a vice president for a multibillion-dollar sales organization and had decided to leave.

"You know, I love what I do. I loved the company I worked for. I had believed in what we did. I moved up the ranks and gained more and more responsibility. Sure, there were challenges, yet actually these obstacles were what fed me. You know? I thrived on overcoming obstacles, achieving beyond often seemingly insurmountable odds, and watching my team knock it out of the park year after year. That was great!

"Then, frankly, one day I was asked to do something that went against everything I believe and stand for. It was a terrible moment. As I knew, I was telling them that I wouldn't do it, that I could not stay with this company. It was an epiphany of sorts, and yet I knew I had to stay true to myself—but, boy, what a decision. It had been a great twenty years," he said almost wistfully.

John realized his values were no longer in alignment with those of his company. He chose to stay true to himself, which in that case meant standing tall in the face of certain rejection and what he perceived to be an ambiguous future. His comments brought back my own fears of loss of security, uncertain destinations, and shifting identity.

Though John was an incredibly successful businessman with a proven track record, he confessed, "I am surprised that I actually feel a bit lost, even disregarded by people I have worked with for years. When we meet they seem to dismiss me, as if not being on the fast track means I have little significance, at least to them. I am beginning to wonder: Who am I now that I no longer have my job, my title, and my influential position?"

He pulled the in-flight magazine from the pocket in the seat in front of him and retreated into scanning it page by page, obviously pondering his own question. I returned to *People*, aware that his question echoed for many.

Who Will You Be When You Are No Longer Who You Have Been?

As with most incidental meetings, when we awake in the moment, we recognize a connection. When we feel empathy for a situation, usually the faces looking back at us are or have been our own. I understood that John believed his identity was all wrapped up in who he worked for, the scope of his responsibility, those to whom he reported, the cachet of working for this well-respected company, and his compensation package. He shared his concern and belief that without this company's brand behind him, he did not have an identity at all. Who was he really? How would he introduce himself now? Would anyone think he had any credibility or value? These questions plagued him, and they haunt many of us when who we "think we are" no longer resembles us, even to *us*.

John had made a courageous move. He had taken stock of what he really wanted to do with his life. As he assessed his own values and ultimate goals, determined how he really felt, what he really wanted, and what fulfilled him, he realized that his role in his company no longer fulfilled him or even moved him in the direction of what he truly wanted. Clearly he had made a decision to be true to himself and what he valued yet had not fully realized how such a dramatic change would alter more than just his vocation.

I have met countless people over the years who believe their identity is completely tied to the company for which they work, the level of position and the title they hold, or their perceived role in life. Despite their individual talents and successes, they have internalized that they are "who they have been" and fear a change that focuses on who they are without an obvious label or role identification.

We've all been there at one point or another—divorce, retirement, change of jobs, or losses of spouses or partners. Navigating new beginnings in difficult circumstances is one of the most challenging phases we face in our lives, yet they can become paths to aligning who we have always been with who we still are. We do not control the circumstances and inevitable transitions that come into our lives; yet we do control how we respond to them. He was getting prepared for his next chapter. By getting to know, and often validating, our core identity, we gain self-confidence and a renewed sense of the adventure called life.

John's identity is certainly not tied to his company. He took a risk and embraced the truth that he is a culmination of his life experiences. He learned that staying in alignment with the man he knew himself to be meant finding his own benchmarks of identity, not those as defined by society, corporate America, or the standards of money, status, power, marriage, children, affluence, or influence.

Entrepreneurship, corporate America, community service, stay-at-home parenting, or a completely new and untraveled course may open new opportunities for alignment. Each individual chooses a path that is *unique*. And John's life, however it manifests, will be *his* life. There is no reason for John to lose his identity in this process. In fact, in the process, he may just find himself.

Being Present in the Moment: Moving Toward Alignment

Questions to consider:

- What do *you* want? How do you want to contribute in this life? What is your definition of success? How have you let others define success for you?
- If you lost your current job or what you consider to be your major role, what facets of your character would continue to define you? Would you no longer be who you have been? How would this reveal the "true you"?
- Are you a different person as a professional, a spouse, a parent, a friend, a son or daughter, or a neighbor? What are the core qualities which form the common thread through all these roles you play?

Not in his goals, but in his transitions, man is great.
—Ralph Waldo Emerson

Mr. Fancy Pants

Airport bartenders are psychotherapists to the global road warrior. I am certain they have seen and heard enough dirt to fill a lifetime supply of popular magazines. One glance around an airport bar and the rawest forms of humanity will greet you. Tired loneliness. Stark unhappiness. Arrogant ambition. Giddy success. Empty accolades. Cool condescension. I have been met with all of these human emotions, most often sitting at an airline club bar.

Pulling my wheel-aboard behind me that Friday felt mind-numbingly normal. That little black bag had become an appendage permanently attached to my right arm. After commuting for four years, the routine was like brushing my teeth, except it involved taxi drivers, TSA security personnel, and numerous other nameless faces that kept the planes, trains, and automobiles moving progressively forward.

"Hey," I said wearily as I struggled to secure my bag beside me and hang my tote bag on the back of the stool.

"Well, hey there! How was your week?" John asked, putting a paper napkin squarely in front of me, while pouring some snack mix in a bowl.

"Glad to be heading home."

"What can I get you? The usual?"

"That would be great. Here you go," I said, handing him my credit card to start a tab.

To a weary traveler, something as simple as seeing your name on a limousine driver's welcome card or a bartender's familiarity with your "usual" can put a lift in your step. The feeling of belonging, being recognized, or having some connection is like a warm blanket on a frigid night to the professional traveler.

John was the long-standing barkeep at the La Guardia American Airlines club. He was a crusty codger, probably nearing sixty years old, with a face that could tell a million stories if only his wrinkles could talk. The muffin top around his waist was like a freshly baked popover. His blue shirt's buttons pulled under the stress and threatened to liberate themselves with one unexpected sneeze. John was all business, not only filling glasses with various concoctions of spirits but also providing free therapy for the weary who were seeking escape and unconditional company before boarding flights back to their reality.

For years, on my regular intervals flying through La Guardia, I watched John dispense advice, listen with actively empathetic ears, and provide comfort. At 7:30 on that particular Friday night, tensions were high. There had been weather delays affecting every flight heading west—basically every flight except those headed abroad.

In strutted a tall, aristocratic-looking man decked in a dark European-cut suit complete with Gucci loafers, Zegna tie, and a French-cut white shirt with onyx cufflinks. He was a walking

Gentleman's Quarterly ad, the quintessential metrosexual. As he pulled out the barstool, he was loudly finishing a conversation on his cell phone through his Vulcan-like headset.

"Fine. Fine. I get it. *I get it.* You want more. It never stops. You know, Cheryl, all you do is push, push, push. When is it ever going to be enough? I will be home when I get home."

He pulled the earpiece out with a quick movement as if he were swatting a mosquito and slammed it onto the bar, shaking his head and mumbling to himself.

John entered the drama from stage right.

"Hi. Sounds like you could use a drink. What can I get you?"

"Bourbon. Knob Creek. Neat. Double."

"Coming right up. Help yourself to some snacks on the corner. Want a water back?"

"No, thanks."

Before John could even put the drink down, Mr. Fancy Pants launched into his tirade about his high-powered position as an executive vice president of a multibillion-dollar, publicly traded technology company. He was careful to speak loudly enough for other interested parties to hear how important his position was. He had been traveling for the past two weeks on a global product launch and was heading home to his wife and three children, ranging in age from eight to eighteen.

He had been on the phone with his wife who, from his perspective, was performing her version of a domestic deposition. He shared that he had amassed a small fortune totaling considerably more than $25 million through several executive positions and taking a few companies public in the dot-com era. Yet his wife wanted him to continue to work.

"She just wants more, more. We have more than enough to live comfortably, to put our children through school, and to travel first class to anywhere we want to go. Frankly, we want for nothing. We have homes in Aspen, Austin, and Saint Croix.

"What else does she want? I don't really know. She loves being able to say she is married to the 'EVP of XYZ Company,' and being able to associate in those circles. You know she wants the designer clothes, the newest Lamborghini, and the largest diamond at the dinner table. Yet I am doing all the hard work and logging these hard hours, not her. She just pushes and pushes—nothing is ever enough."

He paused to gulp his drink.

"You know, sometimes I think she stays with me just because of the money. She gave up her career as an attorney when we had the children. Damn it, I really wish someone would love me if I lived in a tent! Why the hell am I telling you this?"

"Would you love you if you lived in a tent?" John asked, disregarding the last question.

The pregnant pause of all pregnant pauses filled the space. Several of us, listening intently while acting as if we were grossly involved reading the latest *Entertainment Weekly* magazine or *Wall Street Journal*, took deep breaths, waiting for the answer.

"I don't know. Isn't that sad? I thought I liked myself. I used to love the thrill of learning and growing in my job. I used to love the feeling of power, promotion, and public admiration. It just doesn't work for me anymore. What drives me now at age fifty-five is not what used to drive me. Does that make any sense?"

"Sure it does. You know, when you were describing what your wife wants, she sounded a lot like the person looking back at me. Look at what you have on. Listen to how you talk about your success. You sound just like what you said she wanted. We all change and grow, so what gives, man?"

Those of us sitting around the bar caught ourselves sharing wide-eyed glances, amazed at the wisdom and courage of these questions coming from John. What transpired next was nothing short of amazing.

"Easy for you to say. Are you doing what you really want to do? I mean, come on. Are you telling me that you would choose to tend bar at an airline club?"

Calmly, without even a whisper of hesitancy, John answered, "Well, yes, actually I love what I do. You know why? Because I choose to like it. I'm me. I know I am not a CEO or a hotshot lawyer. I serve food and drink to weary travelers, and yet, I meet some really great people. Make a fair living. Hey, and you know what? At the end of the day, we can't take anything with us anyway. What I have is today—this conversation—my time with you. That's really it."

Mr. Fancy Pants's balloon was suddenly pricked with the pin of perspective. One could almost see him deflate as he looked intently at John.

After several seconds of silence, Mr. Fancy Pants offered meekly, "Well, thanks for sharing that with me. Sorry if I came across too harshly. It has just been a really hard day."

"Hey, that's OK. In my line of work, it is hard to get me ruffled. I just hope you find what you are looking for. You know, the first step for someone else to love you if you lived in a tent is for you to love yourself if you lived in a tent. Sure hope you will go after what you really want in this life."

John made the rounds of the bar, checking on his customers. For those of us lucky enough to have been within earshot of that unlikely conversation, we had been served more than enough.

When Values and Success Collide

In "The Pied Piper of Hamelin," the Brothers Grimm tell about a disaster in Germany back in the late 1200s. A man came to Hamelin claiming to be a rat-catcher. The people promised him payment for killing the rats infesting the town by the thousands. So he took a pipe, attracted the rats by his music, and lured them to the Weser River, where they all drowned. Despite this success, the people reneged on their promise and did not pay the rat-catcher.

The pied piper left but returned several weeks later, while the inhabitants were in church. He played his pipe again, this time attracting the children of Hamelin. One hundred thirty boys and girls followed him out of the town, where they were lured into a cave and sealed inside. Most versions of the story say that only two children survived.

Sometimes we, too, may feel as if we have been tricked into following the pied piper into a "cave" lacking fulfillment, joy, and purpose. We can easily become mesmerized by the "pipe music" and trappings of our world. Business practices have honed the game of hooks and golden handcuffs. Standing firm in your values while keeping your job is not for the faint of heart. Mr. Fancy Pants was facing this very dilemma.

As individuals, business leaders, and parents, we all have the potential to be true to ourselves and still keep the interests of those we influence at the forefront of our minds. In fact, being aligned between the goals we have and those of our employees, our shareholders, and others in our lives is the key to having sustainable success—by all measures.

We have the opportunity to create the lives we want. Often that may require having the courage to make the hard calls: when to "cash out," when to choose a different career, and when to say no to a set of values which no longer reflects our own. Years ago, I asked the father of a dear friend how he would define integrity, and he answered, "The courage to stand behind your convictions regardless of the consequences." For a successful west Texas man, alignment was as simple as that.

Which of our values are simply nonnegotiable? Which will become the cornerstones on which we build our business and our lives? Those values, which manifest into behaviors, ultimately define our success. Our behaviors and actions become our character, which ultimately creates our destiny. Weaving our values, what is truly important to us, with how we spend our time leads us toward *alignment*.

Being Present in the Moment: Moving Toward Alignment

Questions to consider:

- Which of your values is non-negotiable?
- Would you love yourself if you lived in a tent?
- What is the "it" you are striving for in life?

At the center of your being you have the answer;
you know who you are and you know what you want.
—Lao-Tzu

47

Crossing the Wall

Ice-cold champagne doused my face and hair, and uncontrollable, happy arms wrapped around me like drunken tentacles as we swayed to the Glenn Miller music. Singing made-up lyrics to familiar tunes, strangers paired into dancing couples. We did not know each other, yet we shared a common bond—the Fourth of July. Americans from all walks of life were celebrating in the center of the metropolitan industrialized city of Berlin.

The night was pitch black, and the stars were as close together as Christmas tree lights, illuminating the sky. The only artificial light came from the inverted dim streaks from the music stands for the small jazz combo. There was a prideful spirit linking us together like a colorful macramé belt woven from strong fibers of various origins. The memory of this night is branded on my soul.

The following morning, Sally, Mike, and I, the happy-go-lucky threesome, awakened to a gray, bleak sky. We were heading into East Berlin, behind the Iron Curtain, and were determined to go despite the ominous weather looming.

"Ready?" Mike called to me, interrupting my thoughts while downing a cup of strong coffee in the hotel cafe.

"Yeah, is Sally?"

"I'm coming. Sorry, just had to grab some more money," she yelled as she rushed into the hotel lobby.

As we boarded the first of several buses, my mind wandered back to my hometown on this holiday weekend. Surrounded by familiar faces, my family was probably at the lake house with barbeque smoking and congregations of friends arriving with plates of potato salad and ice chests of beer. They were celebrating freedom so often taken for granted.

Arriving at Check Point Charlie brought me abruptly back to reality. This was the place two Europeans had died earlier that year by seeking a world they knew virtually nothing about—except that it represented freedom.

The sight of several towers populated with guards aiming machine guns at anyone crossing this chasm without official clearance reminded us where we were. As we stepped hesitantly inside, a stern guard locked it behind us. We were escorted to the small concrete building and handed over to another set of guards. After a stringent sorting of our purses, validation of our passports, and gentle body frisking behind a privacy curtain, we were forced to exchange currency into East Berlin coins and paper bills.

We set out on foot into what appeared to be a rather ordinary city. We saw tall buildings, cars impatiently honking to get through stagnant traffic, and busy people rushing down the side-walks. After a morning of exploration, we stumbled upon a small shop. As we opened the door, a melodious chime invited us into yet another world.

A tent of dust enclosed everything, dulling all sense of color and texture. A cloying, musty odor permeated the atmosphere.

Light seeping through the thin silk lamp shades created mysterious figures on the cracked plaster walls. Candles, melted into unique caricatures, framed a priceless collection of bisque dolls. A mottled mirror reflected a distorted image of an upright piano sitting majestically in one corner of the dingy room. I was drawn to the darkened deteriorating sheet music lying on the yellowed ivory keys: "Moonglow."

A husky voice with a thick accent cut into the air as she emerged from a back corner. "May I help you?"

Startled, I answered quickly, "Oh, no. We are just looking."

I watched as she turned and crept back to her secure little corner. She was stooped over like a fishhook and leaned on a crude wooden cane for support. There was a rocking chair with a crumbling book in the seat. A small oscillating fan made a humming noise. On the chest behind her was a cluster of black and white photos placed on a dingy doily with an eerie masterpiece of cobwebs stretching from the chair to the bureau.

Hesitantly I asked, "Is this your family?"

With a tired, winded sigh, she replied, "Yes. They are my parents, their parents, and my brothers and sisters."

I inched closer to her. She turned to face me, revealing skin like a map of tormented trails. Her thin white hair held in place by a brown hair net resembled an albino checker board.

"Oh," was all I could muster.

"Yes. We are Russian Germans. My grandparents and parents were banished by Stalin. My husband and I came back to Germany after we married. My brothers and sisters were killed in the second war. I have cousins on the other side I have not seen in years. This is what is left of our family's possessions, and I buy from other families to sell, too."

"I am sorry."

"I have been lucky. I have lived long and seen many changes. I have learned. Loved. It is enough."

I stood there feeling insignificant. She had lived through horrors I tried, but failed, to imagine. She weathered them, learned from them, and had been resurrected from them with a grateful spirit.

Extending my hand to this woman, I smiled meekly and thanked her for sharing with me. I wished her well and made my way to the door, eager to leave and reticent to go. The rest of the day was distorted as if viewed through glasses with the wrong prescription.

Abundance, Scarcity

I wonder if this woman lived to see the wall come down. I hope she was able to reunite with her cousins lost to her for so many years. What struck me about her was her unwavering sense of gratitude and abundance despite enduring incomprehensible losses. My perspective was forever changed due to this meeting.

When she said "it was enough," I thought of how so many of my generation simply cannot get enough. We want more. We want bigger, rarer, more exotic, and more exclusive. The more perceivably unattainable, the more attractive it is. And we want it *now*.

This woman was content and even joyous. Her life was simple by our standards. She was surrounded by her past and was continually bolstered by the richness of those memories. It seemed she embraced the "half full" philosophy versus a "half empty" perspective. So many of us believe that we "are not enough," don't "have enough," or can't "get enough." She found pleasure and wealth through her adventures, not through the acquisition of things.

The items accumulated in her past were providing the means for her life. They were literally the means to the end, not the end. There was no bitterness for the inequities afforded her family. In these final years of life, she looked upon opportunities for growth with a spirit of gratefulness. There was an undeniable energy around her, as if love were emitting from her very being. I left her presence believing that love was the grout that glued her disparate experiences into a beautiful and joyful mosaic of life. Love once again proved to be the pervasive ribbon tying us together.

Being Present in the Moment: Moving Toward Alignment

Questions to consider:

- How do you gauge what is "enough"?
- Are you looking at your life from a perspective of abundance or scarcity?
- What gave the shop owner the ability to continue living in gratitude, good memories, and joy despite her terrible losses?

Pleasure is always derived from something outside you, whereas joy arises from within.
—Eckhart Tolle

Summer
Bubbles

When I was young, lightning bugs were everywhere. The air in our front yard seemed blanketed by flashing polka dots. Each night, after a rumble-tumble game of kickball, we performed a whimsical ritual of chasing the points of light. The pace of our small town offered a simple childhood rich for making memories like these.

Each summer for as long as I can remember, my sister and I taught swimming. On the first day of a two-week tadpole class at our public swimming pool, we secured the buoys as the children began to congregate around the pool. Like jackrabbits, they hopped to the cool tile surrounding the pool's edge to avoid burning their bare feet on the hot concrete. As they lined up, they resembled a keyboard of black and white keys donning pastel swimsuits. The most gregarious plunged their feet into the water and began to splash. Others stood obediently like little nutcrackers waiting for instruction, as their parents waited nearby. The smell of chlorine and coconut-laced sunscreen was pervasive.

"Hi, y'all! Welcome to the first day of tadpole swimming! We're excited to start two weeks of fun! Everyone on the edge of the pool—just dangle your feet in the water."

Giggling, they began to take their places. All but one.

"Hi! My name is Kristin. What's yours?" I asked, as I walked through the waist-high water over to her.

The corners of her mouth tilted up timidly. "Kim," she whispered, as she backed away from the edge, just shy of the hot cement surrounding the pool.

Kim was about five years old. Her skin was the color of a Hershey bar with texture as smooth as a pair of doeskin gloves, in stark contrast to her hot-pink, one-piece bathing suit. She had a dozen short pigtails secured with purple and pink plastic rubber bands around her head. She tightly clasped her white swim cap between her hands.

"Hi, Kim! Love your pink suit! Is this your first time to swim?"

She nodded as her marble-sized brown eyes fearfully focused on mine.

"Oh, this'll be such fun! The water feels so cool after being in the hot sun. Come sit here on the side, and let's dangle your feet in the water." She slowly tiptoed to the side and gingerly sat on the edge, letting her feet slip into the water.

"Now, doesn't that feel good? Want me to help you get your cap on?" She nodded sheepishly, and I tugged and pulled to get all the piglets under the rubber cap while she sat with her eyes glued to mine. Her hands tightly gripped the rolled tile edge of the pool.

"There! Now, want to get in?" She shook her head firmly back and forth.

"That's OK. We can sit here and just feel the water. Would that be all right?"

Her back slumped in relaxation and her rigid grip eased. I began to cup my hands and trickled cool water over her legs and arms. She giggled as it dripped down her back and her arms. The water beaded quickly as the hot morning sun drank the excess. I talked to Kim about nothing as she looked down into the pool and at my hands as they doused her repeatedly with cool water.

"Ready now? Just put your arms around me," I encouraged after quite a while, and then extended my arms to her. She stretched out to me with a combined look of dependence and fear. Coming onto my chest, she wrapped her legs around my waist tightly while her arms circled my neck. Her cheek pressed mine, and I felt her soft breath on my ear. I backed into the pool carrying her with me. Her little hands clung to me with more strength than I expected. For an hour, I carried her weightless body around the pool as she grasped me like a new doll on Christmas morning.

The first few days we repeated the same routine as Kim got used to the water. Gradually, Kim began to enjoy the cool ripples, and she let go long enough to make small waves with her hands in the pool.

We shared small snippets of conversation as we glided through the water day after day. I learned she was the youngest of five children. Her oldest sister was fourteen and in junior high school. Her big brother was the one who walked her to the pool each day. She told me her daddy was not at home anymore and her mother worked at the Piggly Wiggly on Grand Avenue checking groceries. They lived in the east part of town in a two-bedroom home. She shared a room with her two sisters, and her brothers slept on a fold-out couch in the basement. She loved to play with her brother's Lego sets and dress up her sister's dolls.

Her favorite color was pink, and she wanted to be a teacher when she grew up.

"Kim, how'd you like to learn to blow bubbles today?" I asked as we swirled around the pool a few days later.

"OK," she said quietly.

"Let's take a deep breath, squeeze our eyes tight, and blow the air out our noses. Ready?"

She nodded and under we went. When we bobbed back up, she blinked her eyes several times and wiped her face with her hands, revealing a toothy, surprised smile. Her grin looked like a picket fence missing a few key rails. She gurgled, "That was fun. Can we do it again?"

Bobbing and blowing. Bobbing and blowing bubbles. The rhythm from that summer long ago is strangely familiar today. We hold our breath. We close our eyes. We bob. We blow out slowly.

Together we practiced this repeatedly over the coming days, playing our horn concertos under water. Submerged, Kim became a master musician. Louis Armstrong would have been proud.

On the last day of our class, energies were high. The euphoric sound of children's laughter anticipating the end of the two weeks was contagious. Kim was at one end of the line of students, at the corner of the pool.

"OK, class. Let's get in the water now. Today, to begin, we're going to practice holding our breath, putting our face in the water, and kicking to the side of the pool."

As the other children jumped into the pool, Kim looked for me. I walked through the ice-blue chlorine to the corner of the pool. Kim reached out to me and jumped into my arms, smiling broadly. Her fear was gone. She grasped my hands, put her head in the water, and began to kick her skinny brown scissors.

When we had gone the width of the pool, she looked up at me, breathless, and pulled herself around me like a wet towel, suspending herself by locking her legs around me. She hugged me tightly and said, "I love you, Miss Kristin. I can swim! I can swim!"

A small moment on a grand scale.

Connection Breeds Trust and Courage

I have no idea why this story, among the many stories of children I have taught over the years, stuck with me. Perhaps Kim's vulnerability or her willingness to take a risk or her courage in trusting someone she had never met caused this one to linger. Or perhaps this success was the first time I realized the real impact we can have on others' lives in the simplest ways. There was such power through our connection that we were both changed through this experience. Regardless of whether Kim remembers that swim class, or me, the moments we shared changed us both.

Connection between individuals is the reason we are here. We are wired for interaction with each other. Kim connected with me at an innocently visceral level. She showed her fear, exposed her vulnerability, and had the courage to rely upon a complete stranger to learn how to swim. Through her growing courage, she forged the bridge that led her to the other side of the pool.

In our daily lives, we are quite similar to Kim. When we lean into our most scary experiences and show our most human vulnerabilities, we build bridges with others. Paradoxically, we need courage to show our fears and our imperfections. At our root level, we want and need to be seen and heard as our most authentic selves, not defined by societal standards, learned expectations from our childhood, or other behavioral norms of the world.

Sometimes folding into the masses as a watered down, homogenous version of who we really are seems easier. Yet we become our most liberated and powerful when we let go of who or what we think we should be and wholeheartedly embrace and celebrate who we really are. We become real.

On a physical and figurative level, Kim let go. She got into the water, took hold of another person's hands, and risked failing—but she didn't. The other person embraced her, helped her float, and supported her, bobbing and blowing bubbles. She took the first vulnerable step in learning how to swim, with no guarantees. The result was a joyful experience with another human being.

At her young age, Kim leaned into her fear, showed her inadequacies, grasped hands with another, and came through on the other side. Our meeting was not accidental; neither are our other incidental interactions. They are all part of this human music. Through the delicate duets we sing with each other, we are divinely inspired to learn and grow.

I don't know what happened to Kim. I never saw or heard of her again. I do know she can swim and is no longer afraid of the water. Kim's story continues to teach the power of vulnerability, the courage to face our fears, and how trust in others can build unlikely bridges connecting us.

Like the many lightning bugs in my hometown front yard, Kim found the potential to become her own point of light in an often dark sky. Fear was eliminated through trust in another. What person may cross our paths today from whom we can learn and whose life we can touch? These interactions may appear seemingly small, but the ripples can go on forever.

Being Present in the Moment:
Moving Toward Alignment

Questions to consider:

- What factors into your decision to trust another person and take a risk with no guarantees? Have you hidden behind masks of who others think you should be?
- What holds you back from taking off your masks and letting the "real you" shine through?
- How do you treat those who reach out to you and show their vulnerabilities? How open is your heart toward others different from you, or who approach a situation differently than you do?

We cannot live only for ourselves. A thousand fibers connect us with our fellow men; and among those fibers, as sympathetic threads, our actions run as causes and they come back to us as effects.
—Herman Melville

Black^Out

I've never met a New Yorker I didn't like. Several years ago I was in the middle of facilitating a large leadership development workshop on the thirty-seventh floor of the midtown Citibank building. Suddenly there was a muffled backward swooshing noise, like an airplane engine cutting off when pilots are going through their tests before take-off.

Nonchalantly I said, "Sounds as if the air just went off. Shall I just continue? I'm sure they will get someone to fix it soon. We don't need lights with all these windows. Let's just keep going."

The sixty souls looking back at me did not share this sentiment. Their faces were painted with primary colors of fear and concern as they looked around at each other anxiously. Then a breathless, panicked voice, which clearly had not been to crisis management school on how to minimize panic, came over the intercom: "Evacuate immediately! Evacuate immediately! Do not take the elevators. Proceed immediately to the nearest stairwell."

Naïve and numb, I casually picked up my briefcase and gathered my belongings. Several of the participants in the workshop turned into overprotective papa bears, hovering around me and telling me to "step on it" as only true New Yorkers can. Their taut, serious expressions began to scare me. I heard one of them whisper, "Just like 9/11." Another whispered back, "Stay focused, stay focused." They did not leave my side as we walked down seventy-five flights of stairs along with thousands of others exiting the building.

When we reached the sidewalk, we realized the problem affected more than just our building. Vertical rows of hot human flesh ten deep created a whirling dervish of activity.

As we learned of the power gridlock that paralyzed the city, a small ad hoc group made our way to an open air café adjacent to a nearby hotel to wait it out. We had no idea this would continue for days and expected to enjoy a short cocktail hour before power resumed returned to normal.

"Hey. My name is Kathy, and I'll be taking care of you today. You guys OK? We have a limited menu, but we will do what we can to serve you." The young waitress could not have been more than twenty-one years old and looked like a blonde version of Pippi Longstocking, one of my favorite fictional characters growing up—lanky, freckled, wearing long braids tied with little pink ribbons. Her Brooklyn accent was easy to distinguish, even for a southerner.

"Thanks! We would love some bottled water. What can you serve in the way of food?" a young man from our group of strangers asked.

"Oh, I am so sorry. We're all out of water. It was the first thing to go. We do have a nice selection of wine still and a few soft drinks left. We only have snack foods to offer, I am afraid, but they are on the house. Let me bring those to you and also the wine list."

A few moments later she returned with the wine list and the mother lode of miniature sacks of corn chips, popcorn, cheese curls, and potato chips. "We'll have a bottle of the Chateau Montalena and five glasses," Denise, a young professional woman in our group, ordered quite abruptly.

"I'll have that right out. Just give me a minute."

Minutes later, to my astonishment, as Kathy poured and Denise took a sip, she retorted, "It is warm! This is totally unacceptable. Do you not have any cooler? I'm sending this bottle back. It is simply not drinkable."

I was horrified, embarrassed, and angry that anyone would respond in this manner under normal circumstances, much less when several million people were clearly facing a collective catastrophe.

"No, I am sorry. This is all we have. I don't even have any ice to offer you."

Denise barked her dissatisfaction with a smug voice sounding just like the tone of Mrs. Upson, of the Upson Downs, from *Auntie Mame*. She and her posse said their hasty good-byes, pushed their chairs back noisily, and bristled out the door. I am amazed at how a sense of entitlement surfaces despite the universal levelers presented in challenging circumstances.

Minutes crept into hours. Gas, cash, and water grew in value as no ATMs, gas, or water pumps functioned. My Girl Scout training, coupled with my father's insistence of always being prepared, made me the most popular waif amongst our group. I had travel candles, a flashlight, plenty of cash, and moist towelettes in my purse. I was happy to note that these assets trump a 36-24-36 figure as a magnet to the male species in a power outage.

Kathy, our waitress, stayed with us for more than twelve hours. Few could leave the city as the subway was not running.

We chose to stay at the café as well. The option of walking up fifty flights of stairs to our rooms, with no air conditioning or lighting other than the candles hotel management placed in the stairwells, was as appealing as a bikini waxing.

Kathy was a hero that night. I watched as she bused tables serving little more than lunch-size sacks of corn chips, warm wine, and a friendly face. Most people's cell phone batteries had died hours before, and the sound of conversation could be heard between human beings in the same room. There was little car traffic, and the typical New York sounds of taxi drivers honking and sirens blaring were eerily absent. The night was dark and deep. It was as if a hidden door had been opened to a secret dark room in the city, except the entire city was that room.

We were without power for almost three days. Never before or since have I felt so connected to millions of strangers. Street vendors gave away free water, young people offered their seats to the elderly, and native New Yorkers helped tourists find their way. Random acts of kindness were as contagious as yawns. Everywhere I looked, there were do-gooders doing good.

I watched hundreds of Kathys reach out to strangers in need. Through this experience, I was reminded that when a crisis strikes, it can bring out the best or the worst of our human condition. How we respond is our choice.

The Good, the Bad . . . the Connected

Being stranded in New York reaffirmed my belief that we human beings are all interconnected. Just as a net is formed through tightly sewn stitches, we form the net of humanity. Its strength is determined by our individual and collective stitches and knots and our awareness of our interconnectedness. I watched in amazement how protective and concerned most of us were of one another. We formed tight connections under dire circumstances.

Those who chose to be more self-absorbed and noncharitable became their own weakest link. The gift of building human connection is, of course, true in every aspect of life, not just when faced with tragedy or adversity. Often difficult circumstances simply shine the light on the most basic human conditions so that we see more clearly our capacity to love, as well as our moral failings, such as those manifested in New York by Kathy and Denise.

I also reaffirmed that when we align to the whole of humanity, we take off the blinders, allowing us to embrace fully the experiences of life. These events, incidental, unplanned, and often seemingly out of order, are not accidents. They are divinely choreographed as part of some giant universal waltz in which we are the dancers. Awareness and appreciation of these happenings teach us about ourselves. Being conscious and awake to these chance experiences will ultimately influence how we choose to live our individual lives and will become the strength and future of our world and our existence.

Being Present in the Moment: Moving Toward Alignment

Questions to consider:

- What "chance meeting" in a stressful situation has altered your perspective of life?
- Does your sense of centeredness stay intact when you encounter a crisis? What do you rely on to maintain this sense of alignment?
- How do you engage with others? Do you choose self-preservation, or do you reach out to help?

You give but little when you give of your possessions.
It is when you give of yourself that you truly give.
—Kahlil Gibran

Angel
with an
Iron Spirit

Sometimes we are lucky enough to realize when angels cross our paths. They blow bubbles into our consciousness without our realizing their buoyancy until much later. They are often not mystical or saintly in the traditional sense, yet the music they sing is memorable in ways not of this world. Sara was one such angel.

I met her while interviewing for an executive position in the fast-paced, no-nonsense world of technology. Her smile was like a beam of light streaking through a cracked door in a dark room. She had a lilt in her voice that reminded me of children's giggles when they are trying to catch their breath from a deep belly laugh. It was laced with a simple, syrupy southern accent, yet peppered with scrappy intelligence.

She was seated behind the large commanding desk and wore a large, bright yellow silk flower on her lapel. I admired the posy for its clear message yet was somewhat disdainful of the fashion faux pas.

"Hello! You must be Kristin!" she said with warm confidence. "They are expecting you. You look great! Just let me tell them you are here. Have a seat."

"Thanks so much," I responded with a bit of nervous energy. I watched her welcome a few others and play switchboard to a few phone calls with quiet competence.

"Good luck—just be yourself," she said cheerfully as the elevator doors opened to reveal the executive assistant who was to take me upstairs to the inner sanctum.

That was our first meeting. No fireworks or voices from heaven, just a typical interaction with the woman at the front desk.

I accepted the executive position in the company a few weeks later and moved forward with my hundred-day plan. I needed a permanent executive assistant and posted the position internally and externally. I narrowed the pool to several candidates through the help of our human resources department. One was the woman from the front desk.

As the door to my office opened, here came Sara speeding through on her motor scooter, this time with a bright red poppy on her lapel. My face must have read like a front page headline: "You are in a wheelchair! What's wrong with you?"

Without a second of hesitation, Sara filled the missed beat with an ease which can only come from practice: "I see you didn't realize I was in a wheelchair. One of the benefits of a high-counter reception desk is that most don't get past my face," she giggled gleefully as if she had really pulled one on me. "I hope that doesn't make a difference to you."

She had me at hello. Her impressive resume of successful entrepreneurship and work in the state capitol for the senate aside, there was just something about her that drew me to her. Call it an energetic vibration. My hiring decision raised eyebrows at all levels within the organization. Many actually said they thought I had lost my "ever-lovin' mind." Others thought I was suffering from tender-hearted naiveté in the critical field of judgment. Sara had a progressive form of multiple sclerosis. She was married to a successful man who suffered from a myriad of illnesses as well. She drove herself to work every day with a hand-operated van fully equipped with a motorized ramp so she could wheel herself in and out without assistance.

She had lived many lives before we met. She had run a successful chain of hair salons before her disease progressed to the point where she could not stand or have full, extended use of her arms. She had no children despite many attempts and just as many miscarriages. Her physical stature may have been weak, yet her spirit was iron.

Her increasing incapacities raised the potency of her presence, as few felt sympathy for her. If anything, we felt embarrassed or in some cases defensive with the increasing awareness of how our own frailties dimmed in light of hers. Her life was like a giant fun house mirror that distorted what we thought was important and reflected reality.

Sara became an integral part of my team. Her intuition and judgment of people were infallible, even if only gauged from a ten-minute phone conversation. She became our gatekeeper, master cheerleader, juggler of resources, and maternal figure. She insisted on personally delivering lunch to us every day, driving her van to the various eateries in the area and bringing it back to us, giving an entirely new meaning to the phrase "meals on wheels."

Her box of rocks seemed so heavy to us. We watched with as much curiosity as awe. Her life was so rich with humor, and she was even cavalier when facing serious inconveniences, if not life-altering game-stoppers.

Tequila with the team was an elixir on more than one celebratory evening when Sara was the jester. She was never martyred or pitiful. For two years, our global team closed business, negotiated career-changing contracts, and continued to reach higher. We went through many tough trials together, and our team wove strong bonds with each other.

These years were cactus-riddled for Sara. Her MS progressed; she had monthly chemo treatments to try to ward off the insidious effects. Her husband continued to fight his own medical battles, which had finally resulted in admittance to the hospital with severe liver failure.

"Kristin, you need to come out here. Something has happened. Sara is on the phone and is inconsolable," whispered a coworker at the door to my office.

I rushed to her desk to find her trembling, barely able to hold the phone with her soft, dainty hands so pummeled by her disease.

"Oh, Kristin," she wailed with a desperate emotion we hear only seldom in our lives. "He is dying. They want to put him on hospice. He only has a few weeks."

She dissolved like weak Jell-O in water. Then within what seemed like only minutes, she solidified with resolve from which I never saw her waiver. We nursed her husband through hospice and watched him evaporate into a seventy-pound tan wrapper of bones and organs. On a beautiful sunny day, we memorialized him in an outside ceremony with our core team present, enveloping Sara. We felt we just reflected Sara's putting her arms around us.

The following week, life continued. We returned to our hamster wheels and Sara to hers. When she was asked how she was doing, the words echoed through the halls again and again:

"I am just fine. My husband is so much better off now. This is just life. We learn from every experience. We don't have to like it all; we just get through it all."

Goodness.

If life is a pool into which pebbles are thrown and ripples result, Sara's ripples are still rolling. At dinner with the CEO of this company, who has remained my friend, I learned just how. His career has continued to be materially full, and he has progressed to even loftier positions. What he said to me that night was not what I expected.

"You know, Kristin, the success I have experienced has been rewarding. However, one of my most cherished thoughts is when you reminded me that the reason I was to be a servant leader and a benevolent CEO was to provide a worthwhile community in which people can work and contribute. You told me one of the greatest things I had done in my prior role was keeping Sara gainfully employed despite the insurance exposure and other challenges. You were right. Not only for what we provided Sara—just look at what she gave all of us."

The tsunami from a single pebble.

Several years later, new leadership at the company took over, and Sara's oasis was drying up. She was let go and would be on disability as long as those benefits held out. As if her challenges had not been sufficient, she was diagnosed with breast cancer and underwent the most radical of procedures.

The last time I saw Sara, we laughed hysterically over cold Negra Modelos. She had just told me that she had opted not to have reconstruction and didn't want to spend the money on expensive prosthetics, so she simply bought a huge sack of bird seed and built her own. Her only hope was that an Alfred Hitchcock moment was not in her future.

Looking back on our experiences together, that was classic Sara—hilarious humor through hardship. Steel framed by faith. Lust for life. We shared the same favorite movie, as she would say, "*Auntie Mame*—the Rosalind Russell version, not the others." She relished life's banquet and approached each day as if it were her last, as perhaps only those who have faced mortality truly can.

Our company's culture never fully embraced the power offered by her example; yet there are a few of us who will carry the image of Sara speeding down the halls of our company in her motor scooter at lightning speed, with a posy on her lapel, living her "can-do" spirit.

Celebrating Mortality

Sara's approach to life is a living testament to embracing and living in the moment. Life on earth is finite. Each of us has the choice of how we spend that time. Sara's experiences continue to reinforce to me the power of those choices. She realizes, perhaps more vividly than most, that her moments on this planet are precious. Certainly she could cower under the pressures of illness, incapacitated mobility, looming financial pressures, and the grief associated with loss. She does not.

Instead, she chooses irreverent humor to face the audacities of life. She chooses to place value on the lessons she is learning through all her life's experiences. She relishes showing compassion and interest in others. She gives unconditionally and, in some cases painfully, just because she wants to. For her, alignment is that simple. Her physical capabilities notwithstanding, she is fully attuned to her purpose in life. Her divinely fueled capacity to support and offer love, despite ultimately having the use of only one hand and arm, brings new meaning to alignment against all odds.

Many coworkers at the company were incredibly financially successful at young ages. At the advent of the dot-com explosion, there were hundreds of twenty- and thirty-somethings who had conservatively acquired millions in net worth. Through this business phenomenon and sudden accumulation of wealth, many developed a sense of financial invincibility and a grandiose view of their own business acumen. Many developed a sense of entitlement, and their expectations and demands were grand.

For those willing to look beyond themselves, Sara offered another perspective. Wealth can be fleeting; she lost her ability to sustain her highly successful chain of retail stores due to her health crisis. Life itself can also be fleeting when illness and unforeseen tragedies land upon us, as they did Sara. She taught us that age and health are privileges not to be taken for granted. Despite her misfortunes, she continues to lap up life with joy, humor, and an incandescent spirit.

Sara will not be famous. She will not be recognized for success in a given professional field or noted for her altruistic monetary gifts to community service. She will not be given public acknowledgment for her contributions to humanity, a technological advancement, or taking a company public. She will not have material wealth of any substance. Yet Sara's gifts to the individuals she touched will continue long after she is gone.

Her legacy will be much more than a street or public building named after her or a foundation created in her name. For those who know Sara, her legacy will be the memory of the insatiable hunger with which she devoured the delicacies of life. She taught us that despite what life hands us, we have the opportunity to decide how, and with what attitude, we forge our own paths. She celebrated life and her own mortality as only those who have looked death in the face truly can. Life is finite, and as Sara's life continues to demonstrate, the present moment is all we have.

Being Present in the Moment: Moving Toward Alignment

Questions to consider:

- How do you approach life's difficulties—with joy for the challenge or with bitterness toward your circumstances?
- How does alignment in your life enable you to cope when life throws you a curve ball? How do you call upon the strength of your values to guide you? From where do you think Sara drew her strength?
- What characteristics do you see in Sara that enabled her to see happiness, not hopelessness? How might you apply that observation to your life and the purpose to which you are committed?

We are not human beings having a spiritual experience. We are spiritual beings having a human experience.
—Pierre Teilhard de Chardin

The
Resiliency
of Dandelions

When all else fails, there are few things that a glass of hearty red wine, a thick Texas rib eye steak, and a loaded baked potato cannot fix—at least temporarily. After a tough week at work, my friend and I decided to go to one of our favorite neighborhood cafés. As we settled into our corner table, a woman with cardboard-colored hair tied up in a messy clump strode toward us.

"Hey, my name is Jayne, and I'll be looking after you tonight. I see y'all already have water. May I bring you something from the bar while you look over the menu?"

"We'll have a bottle of your Parallele '45, Cotes de Rhone, please."

As Jayne opened the wine, I asked her if she was new to the café, since we had not seen her there before. We learned she was not new to Dallas, only to this restaurant. She wanted to know more about us, as well.

"I'm from Hot Springs, Arkansas, originally. I have been here for many years, though."

"You're kidding me, really? I always wanted to live in Hot Springs. I love the ponies at the race track. I plan to move there if I can make a go of it. Need to make some money first."

Over the course of the evening and many evenings thereafter, we got to know Jayne. We pieced together from broken bits of dialogue that her life's road had many potholes. It had left her crusted with grit. She had a scruffy way about her. She never hovered, but she could uncannily appear at the perfect time with another glass of wine or fresh bread. She learned her clients as a teacher learns her students at the beginning of a school year. Her manner was unassuming and self-deprecating, yet there was an air of confidence.

One fall night, as we enjoyed a quick bite of supper, we asked for Jayne. We learned she had been in a terrible car accident. She had broken both of her hips, her left femur, and her right arm. Her recovery was going very slowly, and she wouldn't be back at work for several months.

Caught up in my own life, I forgot about Jayne until a few years later. At a popular Italian restaurant in Hot Springs, my parents and I were reading the menu when I heard a familiar voice.

"Hey, y'all." Before she could finish her greeting, I looked up and saw Jayne's quirky grin smiling at us. Her face was furrowed as if a garden rake had dragged across her ruddy face. Her deep-set eyes told hazel stories of hardship. "I made it! Bet you didn't think I would."

"Jayne! It is so great to see you! How *are* you? When did you get here? Have you worked here long?"

Jayne told us about her multiyear recovery, her one-way trip to Hot Springs in her old Volkswagen Beetle, and losing her mother soon after she moved here. The years had continued to pile heavy bricks on her back, yet Jayne's stance was strong and steady. She lived in a small apartment within walking distance of downtown. She had no phone, television, or computer; she lived a simple life.

Each time I was home in Hot Springs, my parents and I made a point to have supper where Jayne worked. She enjoyed cooking and would often bring homemade enchiladas to my parents' home. An unlikely friendship developed. One night, Jayne came to our table with something in her hand.

"Hey. I want to show you something. Take a look—this is my children's book. Just published it. What do you think?"

We knew Jayne had dreams of writing a book, but we had no idea it would actually happen. *Runs Like a Girl* was a charming little story about a young filly striving to become a winning race horse. We were all amazed. She had created all the illustrations herself. She hoped to market her book to racing club gift shops around the country.

"Jayne, this is so cool. Congratulations!"

"Oh, thanks. It is sorta cool." Clearly she wanted to tell us more about her new life. "You know what I'm doing now?"

"Writing another book?" I chuckled.

She shook her head positively. "On Sunday mornings, I go to the Juvenile Hall and work with the kids there. They've had it tough. They're the misfits, you know. No one wants to help them because people think they've done something wrong. Funny thing is, some of them have been put there just because there's nowhere else for them to go. They've been abused or molested, and there is nowhere else in town for them. It's awful."

I realized that sharing this part of her story was important to Jayne and nodded so she would continue.

"I go and talk and listen to them. I am trying to get them to start drawing as I do, and I think it'll help them, too. I want to take their artwork and use it in another book. I think it may give them something to look forward to—you know, a goal. You want to see them? I can come by tomorrow and show you."

The next morning Jayne came to the house and brought the most amazing collection of drawings by these young children. She told the story behind each picture with passion for its artist. The genius of these children's imaginations spawned hope from a most unlikely place. There is no question Jayne will publish this second book and that it will be successful. As she modestly says, "If I can change one little person's life . . . ."

One morning, as I walked through my rock garden, I saw a dandelion struggling to push through a small crack between boulders. All around it, the roses, caladiums, and azaleas were blooming, surrounded with luscious hosta. Without fragrance and alone in its quest, the dandelion still caught my attention. This singular yellow flower sprouted where nothing else would grow. My mind drifted to another dandelion that pushed her way through rocks and gravel. She blooms beautifully and plants seeds for many future springs.

Reaping, Sowing

Viewed by many as a pesky weed, the dandelion offers valuable vitamins and herbs for culinary and medicinal uses. Rough and gritty, Jayne offers loving sustenance to others and makes a difference in her small corner of the world. She, like each of us, did not have to choose this approach. She could have given up and withered amid the drought in her life. Instead, she chose to persevere and give back in her own unique way.

The word that comes to mind when I think about Jayne is "resiliency." What fuels individuals, who, despite ongoing hurdles and obstacles, persevere and continue to choose to give to others? We can learn so much from role models like Jayne.

I know only a few of Jayne's dreams: moving to Hot Springs, writing a book, and helping children who are facing hardship prematurely in their lives. She has achieved each one against what many would see as formidable odds. She believed she could and would achieve these goals. She created a vision of where she wanted to be, charted a course to get there, and then took the first step and many steps thereafter on her road to alignment. The life she is creating gives her fulfilment and is in tune with her talents, passions, and ongoing desire to give back to the world.

Thousands of unspoken heroes have weathered rough storms that inspire because of their resilient spirits and their ability to "bounce back" and endure despite unimaginable odds. Jayne is just one example who crossed my path. Wherever she is planted, she builds a sense of community that encourages people to know they are valued and respected. Whether these are her customers or the children at the detention hall, she attempts to create an environment of trust and open communication. She focuses on what could be, not just what is. This ability to reframe her challenges as opportunities and visualize a positive outcome converts her probable misfortune into good fortune and makes her future unlimited in its blooming.

Being Present in the Moment: Moving Toward Alignment

Questions to consider:

- How did Jayne align her true self to her true goals despite the hardships she weathered?
- What challenge have you faced in your life where your resiliency carried you through?
- What person have you met in an incidental situation who turned out to be more inspiring and accomplished than your initial impression?

Life is what we make it, always has been, always will be.
—Grandma Moses

The Secret of Respect

As he shuffled toward our table, his hands held in a pseudo-Namaste position, he smiled warmly. Bowing slightly, he greeted us: "Good evening. Good evening. So happy you here."

Mr. Tsubaki was a small, wiry man with a white Q-tip of hair. His eyes were tiny slits like inverted parentheses that gave him the appearance of perpetually smiling.

"Hello," my father said, as he rose to shake his hand. "How are you?"

"Things good. Good. Thank you. Thank you. So happy you here." He continued to bow from his waist after every few words, honoring my father in his own way.

"Glad to hear that! You know we love coming here. How is your family?"

We visited with Mr. Tsubaki for a few more minutes before he disappeared to the kitchen to prepare what would be a delightful sensory shower, beginning with warm towels and ending with fresh, juicy orange slices. Each dish placed in front of us was true to its native origin and prepared with an attention to detail rivaling the most diligent dilettante.

The soup was made of the freshest ingredients and served tableside, and the tempura shrimp was like eating fried air. The plates were perfectly presented with fresh garnishes from uniquely carved radishes and carrots to edible flowers. Each member of the family took turns bringing us courses, gently placing them in front of us as if they were fragile works of art.

The Tsubakis made their home in an old Victorian house on Park Avenue. Their family of eight lived on the top floor while their quaint restaurant was on the ground floor. Mr. Tsubaki, we learned, was a famous concert violinist in his home country. He had moved here several years ago to create a better life and education for their six children. Language was an inhibitor, so Mr. Tsubaki opened the restaurant as a way to provide for his family. In a very short time, he had established a popular business known for authentic Japanese food made from the freshest ingredients and for creating a unique culinary experience.

When they first moved to town, the Tsubakis bought a stately house that needed considerable work to bring it up to code. He and his family were not afraid of a little sweat equity and were quite disciplined in their approach to life and work. He had a dream for what he wanted to create for himself and his family and nothing would deter his vision.

A call had come to my father's company: "I am in need of electrical and air conditioning service. New to town. Can you send someone?"

That initial phone call was the match that lit the embers of what would become a longstanding relationship rooted in mutual respect between Mr. Tsubaki and my father. He was given the complete tour of the Tsubakis' home and soon-to-be-business.

Mr. Tsubaki was tremendously proud and equally humble in his demeanor. He carried himself with a quiet air of confidence, building a bridge of trust between him and anyone he met.

He revealed his limited budget, and my father gave assurances that the company could take care of the project. They shook hands as they parted.

Many years had passed since that initial meeting. We frequented Mr. Tsubaki's restaurant regularly. One evening I mentioned to my father how admirable it was to see what Mr. Tsubaki and his family had accomplished.

"Oh, he is a good man. Impressive work ethic. Incredibly resourceful. Unflinching in the service he provides to his patrons. His entire family is devoted to building that business. He worked so very hard to pay our bill. We never told him that we charged him only a fraction of what the system actually cost. We wanted to give him a chance to succeed. Respect and dignity, Kristin. That is what life is all about."

Sharing the Gift of Respect

Mr. Tsubaki and my father shared the basic belief of aligning their actions with their values. Without being aware of my father's gift to him, Mr. Tsubaki built a thriving business grounded in excellence and service to his customers. My father, in turn, was given the gift of seeing his faith in and respect for another rewarded with Mr. Tsubaki's success. Knowing his part in the Tsubaki family's story resonates with me still.

My grandfather taught my father this lesson, and now my father is teaching me. Giving of oneself and one's capabilities with a spirit of pure generosity and love is the joy in life. Genuine giving to others, by definition, is not a self-serving, credit-guzzling experience. It is most joyous when given anonymously without leverage of power or expectation. The individuals and organizations to which my father and mother have anonymously given over the years remain a mystery even to me. Mr. Tsubaki is just one that stands out because of his own Horatio Alger story and the small ripple effect my father's service and invisible protection of another's dignity undoubtedly had on two lives.

Giving the gift of respect and preservation of dignity benefits the giver as much as the recipient. There are hundreds of opportunities to show respect and give dignity to those we meet serendipitously in life. My father understood that how we treat these incidental people in business and in everyday life affects us as much as them. We get what we give in spirit. My father's generosity coupled with Mr. Tsubaki's determination for success testifies to the power of mutual respect and the joy it brings to the giver as well as the recipient.

Being Present in the Moment: Moving Toward Alignment

Questions to consider:

- What lessons can you learn from Mr. Tsubaki's courageous choices and quest for alignment toward a better life in the United States?
- Was there a time you offered an anonymous helping hand to another? How did you both benefit?
- In what ways can you show respect to those who play small roles in your life?

The bond that links your true family is not one of blood, but of respect and joy in each other's life.
—Richard Bach

The Grace to Be Chosen

Before you entered her small cubicle, you could smell the "feel good" hint of rose perfume. Its softness filled the air up and down the aisles of the office, leading you to her.

Her blood-red nails clicked as they hit the keys of the old IBM typewriter. Her black hair was pinned up in a loose bun with tendrils falling around her neck and framing her face as if by accident.

"Good morning! You must be Kristin, the new sales executive working for Ed, right? I'm Pat! Come on in. Welcome! Are you excited?"

I walked into her oasis of family photos, funny magnets, and a small vase of fresh daisies to the right of her vintage black push-button office phone. "Hi! Yes, I am new. I was told to report today by 8:30 a.m. and that you would be my point person for my first day."

"That's right! Now, you just have a seat and let me get your folder, and we will walk through your schedule today." As she stood up, all five foot four of her, she adjusted her floral blouse, which was fitted to accentuate her Scarlett-sized waist, smoothed her pencil-straight skirt, sucked in her stomach, shoved her shoulders back, and proceeded to prance perkily across the hall. She walked with truncated steps like a Chinese woman with bound feet. Her brisk gait made a metronome of her hips keeping track of her tempo.

"Here we go. Now swing your chair over here, and let's see what we have on your roster for today."

That was the first time I met Pat. She was the quintessential executive assistant, like a brunette Dolly Parton straight out of the movie *Nine to Five*. Over the next several years, I learned Pat was feminine steel, flexible and malleable when heat was applied and rock solid when put under pressure. She became a business mother of sorts. Shrewd, savvy, and fiercely loyal.

There were no female executives in the company. The few of us in this field were either naïve or bull-headed—perhaps a combination. Most were trying to emulate men with their blue suits, red bow ties, starched white shirts, and staccato stiff language.

Pat was the antithesis. She accentuated her womanhood with every inch, eyelash flitter, and empowering position for the purpose of persuasion. She was beloved for her sultry sense of self and respected for her iron constitution and her devotion to excellence and customers.

How selfishly the face of fate can claim change with no warning. Hers began with a twitch in her fingertips when she typed. She said her fingers felt as if they were asleep and then waking up with the familiar pens and needles sensation. Initially, she thought she had developed carpal tunnel syndrome. When she one day shared her true diagnosis, it was a dark moment.

"ALS. Amyotrophic lateral sclerosis. Lou Gehrig's disease." The words hung heavily, suspended somewhere between reality and denial; then they landed with a thud in the center of our relationship.

Pat's diagnosis was made before Mitch Albom's book *Tuesdays with Morrie* made an ALS prognosis somewhat familiar. Hers was an unforeseen trip no one wanted to take, but she had no choice. She was on the train, destination known, and her own Auschwitz awaited her.

Pat was a work friend. She was not a person I would call to see a movie or even to have dinner. She was not a contemporary; she was married and had children. Our working relationship was undeniably close prior to the diagnosis; however, the disease was like glue between us. Our bond grew stronger. We were unlikely soul mates.

Her disease progressed quickly. Pat never asked, "Why me?" In fact, during one of the first heart-to-heart explosions we shared, she quietly offered, "I must have been chosen for a reason. I have to believe that and embrace this experience with grace."

And that is how she was. I never saw her waiver from her formidable faith. She would take each day, each tube, and each loss with an unshakable faith in her destiny. She would teach us through her quiet, unspoken strength how to face the unspeakable. We will never fully know, unless we experience it ourselves, what this must have been like for her.

She quickly lost the motor skills in her legs and arms and was forced to make her new world the corner of her couch where she could greet visitors, watch TV, and talk on the phone. Progressively, she lost the ability to swallow and had to have a tube inserted into her stomach for her daily meals.

Within a year she was moved to a hospital bed in the main room downstairs. Her hair turned white and was cut very short. The nurse's assistant had to vacuum her mouth every few minutes because even a small drop of saliva felt like a giant gulp of water drowning her.

Her body became a hard cocoon, and she had no strength to release herself. Small sensations gave her pleasure. She was fond of Chanel No. 5 hand cream that her nurse's assistant would rub on her feet and arms. She said it made her sheets and bed smell real, as if she were "still in the real world." It made her feel womanly again.

Visiting Pat became a part of my routine. I would see her only every few weeks, so the disease's progression was quite notable. Over time, Pat's once vibrant and melodic voice became deep and abbreviated. She was a live mummy encased by her own skin. Her dancing eyes, always bright, still danced, but in my mind, the tempo was a slow waltz, not a rousing tango.

The last few times I visited Pat, she had been relegated to spelling out our conversations on a board with strangely arranged vowels and consonants. The only parts of her body she could still move were her eyelids, and she would spell out her words for me by blinking, one by one, with the help of her assistant.

"Pat, I am so happy to see you. How are you today?"

I A-M F-I-N-E, she spelled out with the painstaking effort of a first grader trying to write on a large tablet with a no. 2 pencil.

I looked at her lovingly, with too much pity, and stroked her arm, as if I could rub away the disease. As she stared at me, her eyes were like bottomless blue holes that held years of experiences too horrible and unimaginable to comprehend and thousands of words not spoken. I offered silly conversation to fill the time and gave her the latest office gossip. Almost two years had passed since she had been forced to leave her job, and yet she still wanted to keep up with the goings-on. Then, without warning, she started to choke. Quickly the nurse's aide came to vacuum her mouth and throat, while Pat looked through me with piercing intensity.

"Pat, I must go now," I said with an awkward discomfort. "I will be back in a few weeks. Love you."

I L-O-V-E Y-O-U T-O-O. D-O N-O-T W-O-R-R-Y. A-L-L O-K. I A-M R-E-A-D-Y.

I bent down to kiss her and leave, looking longingly at the nurse's aide as if to give her my eternal gratitude for being the angel at Pat's side through this last phase of her journey. Once in my car, I breathed a sigh of combined sadness, relief, and guilt. I wanted someone, anyone, as if I were a little child again, to kiss and make all better this sickening, nauseating feeling of utter hopelessness.

A few weeks later, Pat and I spent our last few minutes together. Her black hair that once fell in soft curly tendrils was now a Brillo pad of coarse white stubs. Her long crimson fingernails were now clipped short, and her hands were swollen, resembling fingerling potatoes. Her once petite body was now a spongy mass saturated with fluids slowly hardening like freezing milk. The once fragrant aroma of roses had been replaced with a faint smell of Chanel No. 5 mixed with a medicinal stench.

Pat cut her eyes over to me as her aide led me to her bed. Despite my best efforts, my eyes filled and spilled onto my cheeks. I reached for her hands and held them softly.

H-I. H-O-W A-R-E Y-O-U? she slowly spelled.

"Oh, Pat. I am fine. I am just so sorry," I whispered. Our eyes linked, and not another word was spoken. A whimsical smile came upon my face, and I saw Pat blink twice, the sign for yes. She knew.

Aligning with Grace

Grace fills my memory of Pat. Through her many travails and horrific experiences, she never lost her poise and steadfast strength. She navigated each aborted opportunity of her life with a compass of faith. Her freedoms were taken away slowly and steadily. She became 100 percent dependent upon the service of others, and still her independent spirit remained resolute.

Surely, in her private moments, she experienced fear of loss, death, pain, and the unknown. And yet, never did I see her cower. In the face of death, she figuratively rolled her shoulders back, squared her chin, and boldly moved forward into the darkness. Her unflinching belief that this was her unique road to travel fueled her solidarity. This unwavering will to align the hand she was dealt with sublime grace was one lesson she taught in the last few years of her life.

As her disease worsened, Pat's dependency on others became nonnegotiable. Pat simply had no choice. She was reliant on others for every single aspect of living: for water, daily nourishment, and even swallowing without choking. I watched her oblige these ever-increasing dips into dependency with quiet determination. She taught us that leaning on others did not denote weakness; it may actually strengthen us—and those who help us.

Often we find ourselves traversing uncharted waters. Many factors other than a terminal illness may have a dramatic impact on our lives. Perhaps we have taken on an assignment that tests our capabilities, or we embark on a new career in mid-life. These changes, though exciting, can be frightening. Many times we think we need to "go it alone." Pride often gets in the way of reaching for help. Pat didn't have that option. She was forced to relinquish any false pride and embrace the help of others.

I have many clients, individuals and companies, who are struggling. They may be faced with declining sales, reduced profits, unprecedented layoffs, and lack of job stability for themselves. They are insecure about the future, which breeds more fear, leading to anxiety and often to paralyzing depression. We may not want to burden anyone else with our issues and often do not want to ask for help for fear of being perceived as less competent.

Pat taught us just the opposite. An important step to a person's individual quest for alignment begins with an outreached hand. Each of us brings unique talents and experiences to life and the workplace. Embracing our lives, opening ourselves to the possibilities, and welcoming support from others can clarify and strengthen our perspectives, resolve, and overall approach to life and work.

Being Present in the Moment: Moving Toward Alignment

Questions to consider:

- How do you align the difficult challenges in your life with your strengths, hopes, beliefs, and values?
- When you experience challenges, unfamiliar territory, or sadness, what resources do you call upon for strength?
- What gifts do you receive for taking a risk when you face a terrifying challenge head on? What gifts do you give?

You have to accept whatever comes, and the only important thing is that you meet it with courage and with the best you have to give.
—Eleanor Roosevelt

William's Way

What about going to the grocery store, like traveling, brings out the best and worst in people? We can often learn the truth about shoppers by how and what they buy. Some are always in a hurry and ram their carts past others on the narrow aisles, barely mumbling "excuse me." And there is always that one person who has a jammed-full handheld basket that will invariably get in the "Under 15 Items" checkout line.

One day, while I was browsing the produce section, a chipper voice shouted, "Hey! How're you? Did you know there's a special on watermelon today?"

"Oh, thanks, William," I said, glancing down at his nametag.

"You're welcome. Sure is hot today. Yeah, when I get off, gonna watch the game. Yeah, gonna get off soon. Gonna watch the game."

He spoke with an impediment, and his mouth was full of spit as if he needed to swallow yet could not or did not want to. His lips had a fine crusty outline of white residue at their corners. He stood about five foot eleven with a trim build and a haircut resembling a terrier freshly sheered from the pet parlor—close, cropped, and crew. He was fastidiously stacking the Rome apples, paying careful attention that all the stems pointed the same direction.

I learned that William was what some folks would call "slow." He dressed tightly like a well-wrapped package with the corners correctly creased and held in place with Scotch tape placed on the inside of the paper. He stood tall and thrust his shoulders back at attention like a toy soldier. When he sacked groceries, he had a deliberate process. The canned goods went in one sack, dry goods in another, and produce in yet another. He would double sack eggs, wine, and other glass bottles. He took his job as seriously as a heart surgeon performing an angioplasty procedure. He always offered to carry the groceries, rain or shine, for anyone laden with more than one sack. I became intrigued with William and inspired by his dedication to his job.

"Hey, how're you? Paper or plastic?" He would embark upon some empty banter about the items he was sacking, then wrap his curious questioning with, "Do you want some help out?"

Some customers looked at him with disdain, as his conversational efforts often slowed down his sacking and hindered their hurried pace. They would often leave in a muffled huff, which apparently they thought he did not notice. William would look over at me after one of these interactions, shrug his shoulders, and say, "They are having a hard day. No big deal."

My weekly William meetings went on for years. I began to switch checkout lines just so I could have William sack my groceries, a strange ritual because his lines were invariably the slowest. William would often comment on an item in my basket which could spark embarrassment: "Oh, I see you're buying the extra large sack of Fritos! Don't you live alone? You must be having company!" I might not be having company—I just wanted the extra large sack because I wanted the extra large sack!

If I bought a somewhat unusual item, like fennel, he would say, "What is that?" spawning into a full discourse on how to use fennel, whether it was a fruit or a vegetable, and what its nutritional value was. His questions were unfettered and lacked filters. He wanted to learn. He wanted to engage. There was no false pride; he boldly asked what he wanted to know and fearlessly welcomed the unknown.

When I moved, the grocery store where William worked was a bit too far for me, and I lost track of him. Years later, as I began to check out a new neighborhood store, there he was!

"William! Hey! How are you? I have missed you! Where have you been? It is so good to see you."

"Hey, Miss Kaufman. Yeah, my store closed for renovation. How're you? Sure is hot today. I'm gonna watch the game tonight. Yeah, gonna watch the game later."

Time had not affected William in the slightest. After all these years, his world had remained somewhat constant. The axis on which his life revolved was "paper or plastic." William's physical world was a tiny terrarium, limited in scope, complete with a white apron and nametag.

William's options were limited in some ways. His choices had been curbed by many people's standards, yet I stood there watching this man make kind and worthy decisions on a daily basis. The outer banks of his horizon were the aisles of a grocery store, but within his capacity, he surveyed the entire field of vision. He chose to do a yeoman's job each day with an attention to detail that would amaze the most obsessive-compulsive pointillism painter. He chose to ask questions that may have appeared naïve to many. He chose to continue to learn and be inquisitive despite his limitations. He chose to be friendly and cordial even when the audiences of his affection were rude and inattentive.

As he filled my sacks, I said, "Hey, thanks, William. See you later!"

"You're welcome. Have a good day. See ya later, Miss Kaufman."

As I left the store, I heard a high-strung, bossy voice say, "I am in a *real* hurry. Now, be sure you put the eggs in a separate sack. No, no. Put the paper goods with the canned goods. Now I want you to double-sack the milk. Hurry—I am in a huge hurry!"

I turned and caught William's eye. He winked at me and smiled.

Choosing Our Way

As I enjoyed my friendship with William, I found that one of my long-held beliefs was cemented: *a person's choices create his or her life.* William chooses to serve cheerfully, in his simple way, though he could make other choices on how to spend his time.

Conversely, our choices may lead to personal change and altered priorities. Regardless of what life hands us, the choices born of our experiences lead us where we find ourselves today. Our choices relative to sacrifice, discipline, entitlement, courage, fear, and love become the cornerstones in the lives we create and ultimately the harmony brought from a truly aligned life.

At dinner with friends and colleagues one night, I listened as one individual complained about how life had not turned out the way he had hoped, how he had always tried to do the "right things." He was not where he thought he would be at this point in his life. This commentary created an avalanche of conversation among the rest of the dinner guests. Almost all fell short of where they thought they would be at this stage in their lives. The "could-have, would-have, should-have" discussion took over the dinner table.

We have all heard this conversation many times. We want that promotion. We want another child. We want to retire by age fifty-five. We want at least what our parents had. We want *our* "plans" to come through. We want progress, but we also want the stability of what we "know." We are often too stubborn or scared to let go of our rigid plans or expectations, or we are too blind to see that a new door is already open for us.

Ironically, the new opportunity may be even bigger, better, and brighter than the path we previously traveled. Sometimes we get stuck in a victim mentality of what is happening "to us," we wallow in "what isn't," and we refuse to take back the reins of our lives. We have all been there; some just decide to stay at that party longer than others. The reality is that when tides shift, letting go can create unexpected opportunities. Often we refuse.

We have to let go of those things we cannot change and change the things we can. William has. He may not realize his choices in the same way we do, but he is playing well the hand he has been dealt.

Being Present in the Moment: Moving Toward Alignment

Questions to consider:

- Twenty years ago, where did you envision you would be today?
- What treasured experiences and people would not have been in your life if your expected future had occurred?
- What bit of insight can you recall from an unlikely source—perhaps someone you hardly noticed at the time? Did that experience prompt you to become more alert to the value of and potential wisdom from "incidental meetings"?

It is choice, not chance, that determines your destiny.
—Jean Nidetch

Tragic
Choices

Several years ago, my sister and I thought we would enjoy investing in some lake property. We found a lake cottage on a quiet cove on one of the three beautiful lakes surrounding our hometown. It was a perfect weekend getaway with a spacious wooded lot, a wraparound porch on the second story, and a handsome piece of shoreline. It needed minimal renovation to make it ready to lease, and with its wood-burning fireplace, hardwood floors, and spacious living area, it was an ideal house for entertaining.

We leased it in no time and enjoyed a relatively simple season of steady boarders over the first few years. Landlord newcomer naiveté was sheer bliss.

When our most recent boarders moved out, we placed our leasing advertisement in the local papers. When Larry first came to our office to inquire about the property, he resembled a human beaver. He had a single, large, scraggly tooth standing at attention from the very center of his top gum—not on the left or the right, smack dab in the middle. His receding hairline of black wisps framed two black marbles placed too close together on either side of his hooked nose. He was plainly dressed, and as my grandmother would say, "at least he was clean and shaven."

"Hey, how're you? My name is Larry Jones. Read you have a place for lease. I'm interested in seeing it. I live alone. Has it been rented yet?"

That's how we began. We showed him the property. He told us he built electronics such as grocery store scanners for several privately held grocery store chains. He provided several personal and professional references, all of which checked out perfectly. He signed our contract and assured us that he would pay our rent in cash no later than the third day of each month.

Larry appeared to be the model tenant. In fact, he offered to improve the property by building a rock wall around the lakefront and around our property line—all at his expense. He offered to build a boat dock and continue to improve the landscaping. He was never late on his rent, he kept to himself, and from what we were told, he was a friendly and helpful neighbor. All was rocking along beautifully until my father got a phone call in the middle of the night from the neighbors.

"Joe, you need to come to your daughters' rental property. There are at least a half a dozen federal and state police cars in the driveway. There is a huge bust going down."

"Girls," my father said on the phone the following morning, "we have a problem with your tenant. It appears he was cooking meth in your house. The police have arrested him, and the property is now a federal and state crime scene. The story is on the front page of the paper."

The house was ransacked from top to bottom by the police. Every ounce of metal, from door knobs to cabinet handles to kitchen appliances, had rusted due to the acid from the methamphetamine production. Our fifteen minutes of real estate rental utopia was now a bit of sludge slowly circling the proverbial drain.

"Larry" was one of several aliases he had used over the years. "Darryl" was his birth name, and he had been convicted of dealing drugs prior to moving to our hometown. He had faked his own death a few years earlier by "drowning" in one of the largest lakes in this area. He left his identification, credit cards, and clothes in a boat and virtually disappeared.

The county services proclaimed him dead after a lengthy search, complete with dragging the bottom of the lake; his mother had a memorial service. He surfaced a few years later as Larry, reinvented himself, and built a modest business taking electronic parts from old appliances to build rudimentary scanning devices for small grocery stores.

All the home improvements being made to our property were done on the backs of Larry's drug clients. They paid for their drug habits through the labor and material costs for the improvements at our house. The free enterprise system was operating from the gutter—our gutter.

When Larry was released from jail after the drug bust in our house, we learned he had moved to another small town in our home state. He was again arrested for making drugs in some makeshift location. Knowing he would be locked up for a long time, he swallowed a lethal combination of drugs and died in the back of a police car.

When What Appears So . . .

If this story were not so tragic, it might have made a black comedy. None of us ever suspected Larry of being anything but honorable. We never questioned he would be anything but a steady and reliable tenant. We believed the best of him.

How Larry arrived at this point in his life remains unknown, but his mind was quick and capable of engineering complex feats. What could have become Larry's life had other choices been made? What could his final chapter have been? Why did Larry's path cross ours?

We all could be Larry. Every single one of us has the gift of free will, one of the most important privileges of our lives. It places the accountability noose squarely around our own necks. Despite where we find ourselves in life, we have the ability to choose the direction we want to go.

We also have the tempting option to resign ourselves to a fate we believe has been definitely determined. Many have chosen the course of resignation to what they see as an inevitable situation. Perhaps this was Larry's rationale or a mentality of worn-out resignation.

The phrase "it is what it is" has become our catch-all excuse for where we find ourselves in life. There are situations that "are what they are," and yet there are many others that can be changed. I wonder if Larry simply resigned himself to follow the path of least resistance and the one with which he was most familiar. Sometimes just going with inertia, rather than pushing against and through it, is simply easier.

Ultimately, we write our own stories. Larry's decisions to pursue this path of unlawfulness created the life he led. In our lives, if we believe this is the "only game we can play" or that the "game is over," then it will be over before the starting buzzer has even sounded. Many individuals have been dealt heavy hands and figuratively throw in the towel and resign themselves to their "lot in life." This path may appear to be easier, as in the case of drug-dealing Larry, yet the choices we make ensure our fate.

When we succumb to the temptation of resignation, in whatever form it takes, our fate is sealed. Giving up is not an option for those individuals who want to live their best life and to continue contributing in their most optimal way. Every single one of us has his own sack of rocks; what distinguishes us is how we carry that load.

This experience reminded me that we learn through our mistakes. Never before or since have I been so blatantly deceived. Innocent, naïve trust led to a grave mistake for my sister and me. What did we risk with our decision to lease to Larry? How could we have screened our tenants more effectively? We often get "burned" in relationships and may alter how we engage with others as a result. I have certainly become more inquisitive and often downright cautious when engaging in professional relationships. I still choose trusting other people until they have proven they are not trustworthy. Perhaps my true lesson is that I must realize that the individual will be who they really are, not who I want them to be. Embracing that reality and not projecting my desired expectation on the relationship shines a bright light on the situation.

Sadly, the poignant lesson I learned from Larry was that our choices, his and mine, reveal our values, manifest our priorities, and ultimately determine our life's direction. We gave Larry an honest and unconditional opportunity to live up to his potential. We never presumed anything other than honor and trustworthiness from him, as a person and as a tenant. I believed he had honor within him, yet his choices were weighted by whatever fears and rocks he had carried with him throughout his short life.

Being Present in the Moment: Moving Toward Alignment

Questions to consider:

- When have you assessed another, "judged a book by its cover," and been mistaken?
- How have you maintained trust in others after someone has betrayed your trust?
- How do you respond when friends or colleagues have betrayed or rejected you? What can you learn? What can you teach?

It matters not how strait the gate,
How charged with punishments the scroll.
I am the master of my fate:
I am the captain of my soul.
—William Ernest Henley

Swans and Ugly Ducklings

As we headed for the slopes my travel mates, donned in black Lycra body suits and dark glasses, were Batgirls on skis. I felt like a "wannabe" in my borrowed, brightly colored ski wear as I clumsily waddled from our condo to the lift not one hundred yards away. My travel buddies, black slope barracudas, had headed to a place where the rich and famous played. I had arranged for a beginner's course on the bunny slope.

Once on the lift, sailing above the slopes and watching little figures slide down the mountain, I felt like one of them. This nanosecond of confidence was interrupted when I realized the liberating lift ride was coming to an end. For an instant, I thought it would be a fun escape to just stay on the lift the entire day, but I was thrust off into the snow and found myself sliding onto the little patch where a troupe of tots with their matching hats and gloves assembled. A handsome man skied over to me with a swagger few master even on dry land.

"Hi, you must be Kristin. My name is Mark. I am your instructor."

Of course I am Kristin. I am the only person here over the age of six. "Hi, Mark."

"Is this your first time to ski?"

"No, but not for years."

"Well, you are clearly in shape. You will have this whipped in no time. Ready?"

Boosted by this nonchalant compliment, I nodded timidly. We began our dance slowly with Mark skiing backwards holding my hands and pulling me behind him. He told me to focus on my hips and body frame and all else would follow.

"You were a dancer, weren't you?"

"How did you know that?"

"I can tell by the way you lean into this. Your body is in full alignment, which is so important in dancing and skiing. You will be a fabulous skier. We will be on the green slopes before noon, maybe even the blue slopes this afternoon."

I hung on to his every word. My confidence was building, and as we slid and swayed down the hill, I finally found my legs. He coached me to stay loose and just feel the snow. More than once, I tipped over; he applauded and encouraged me. He said my grit and risky approach showed strength and natural ability.

As we crested the green slope later that morning, we took a quick look at each other, and we were off. He was by my side, cheering my form and speed as I grew plucky and poised. As we came to the bottom of the hill, we laughed, hugged, and celebrated. There I was, puffed up like a Christmas turkey just because I was able to ski down a green slope without falling.

Later, as I started another descent after masterfully disembarking the chair lift—now my new best friend—I began to pick up speed the way my childhood sled, stacked high with three of us, used to do on the steep neighborhood hills after an ice storm. Suddenly I was a reckless runaway, losing all form and balance, splaying my poles into the air as if they could skewer something stable to stop me. I finally slurred to a rough and tumble, squatty stop. My body crunched forward, and my left leg bent backward and popped like a rubber band against the Sunday morning paper. That mouth-watering, lightheaded feeling preempting nausea came quickly. As I sat there trying to gain my composure, thankfully, none of the pretty people pummeling down the hill stopped. That would have been more ego-swallowing humiliation than my bruised self could take. I took several deep breaths and pulled myself up with my poles and stood with my left leg dangling loosely. Debating what to do next, I tried to maintain a cavalier carriage, as if every day people decide to squat midslope to take in the view.

I realized there was no way I could ski down the hill, so I did what any nonchalant seasoned pro would do. I took off my skis, lumbered them under my arm, and began the long walk back up the hill. I waved and smiled at the passersby as if everyone should try a backwards ascent.

"Hey, you! What happened?" yelled a surprised Mark as he skied past with another client. "Are you OK?"

"I'm fine," I said, limping with my left leg bent at a thirty-degree angle, using my tippy toes as a left foot. "Just hurt my leg a little. I'll be fine! I am going to go in for a while and get warm. See you later."

While my Barbie friends skied the slopes the rest of the weekend, I read and met interesting folks in the numerous watering holes at our resort and held on to my image as a graceful dancer. I was a veteran, of sorts, with a war story to tell. I never went back to that ski resort, yet I still like to think of myself as a snow queen ballerina learning to dance *en pointe* for the first time with my own handsome Baryshnikov.

The Slippery Slope of Challenge

This trip to the slopes was not the first time, or certainly the last, when I pursued something I had never before attempted. Perhaps many of us follow the same familiar emotional path when tackling something new: excitement, fear, trepidation, episodic insecurity, resolve, focus, work and more work, and satisfaction.

Despite daunting challenges, most of us move forward. In Colorado, I risked embarrassment, possible failure, and public humiliation to learn how to slide down a snowy hill on two long, skinny slats of wood. I mounted the bunny slopes amid the fearless four-year-olds to learn the basics.

This experience reminded me that we often do not realize how strong we are until our muscles are tested. We do not know the strength of our convictions until they are stretched. There is no doubt in my mind that from the challenges we take on we become stronger, and a better self emerges. I also believe that in the face of our challenges, our most authentic self is revealed.

Often we get stuck in the fear stage. I have worked with many executives who do not want to risk failure, public exposure, or simply making a mistake. Mark reminded me of the power of creating a safe place for growth and experimentation. He encouraged me, gave me permission to fall, and peppered his instructions with disarming humor. By creating a safe environment, he helped my fears diminish and my potential thrive. Here was a man who, with kindness, respect, and trust, encouraged me to try and ultimately to succeed.

In our businesses and in our lives, we can replicate the same safe place that Mark created for me. We can offer unconditional support. We can provide an environment where risks are encouraged and successes and failures are rewarded. Safety creates a freedom within us and between us, and through this freedom, our most powerful talents and ideas are liberated. When we are free, we give ourselves permission to pursue a life of authenticity and alignment. And when we are in alignment, we are our most strong, fearless selves.

Our limiting beliefs can hold us back; our dreams can propel us forward even if we ultimately must attempt a "backward ascent."

Being Present in the Moment: Moving Toward Alignment

Questions to consider:

- How does your sense of alignment factor into the safe place you create?
- What happens to you when you take a risk and fail?
- How can you help lead and support someone else facing a challenge, even if that person must march back up the "slope"?

A ship is safe in harbor, but that's not what ships are for.
—William Shedd

Flavoring
One Corner of the World

The second you open Mollie's door, you crawl into a warm nest filled with the aroma of southern cooking (shorthand for everything fried) and a homespun air of familiarity. As you walk down the hallway of the old bungalow cottage you see the permanent fixtures of Paul and Betty sitting in their booth, cigarettes in hand, large dictionary in the middle of the table, working on their *New York Times* crossword puzzle. Mollie's was our neighborhood eatery, an addictive combination of a southern kosher kitchen, old-shoe faces, and the unique owners, Paul and Betty.

Known for having a world-class Reuben, they also served the best fried chicken livers I have ever eaten. Enriched by the owners' Jewish heritage, the matzo ball soup was straight from Paul's grandmother's kitchen, along with the other recipes that had made Mollie's an institution in our town since Paul's grandmother started it on Central Avenue back in Al Capone's day. Suffice it to say a trip back to my hometown was never complete without supper at Mollie's.

"Hey Kaufmans! How are you doing? Good to see you! Drinks all 'round? Same as always? Be right back!"

Not waiting for an answer, our waitress bustled back to the bar. To say Barbara filled a room would be an understatement. Towering at six foot one, her frame was bent between the shoulders because of the weight around her middle that did more than balance her height. Her voice mimicked a bass drum in a well, the full dollop of crème on her already hefty portion of personality. Her neck resembled a turkey's, the skin drooping loosely under her chin and onto her décolleté moved side to side when she walked. Other than always having a short, updated haircut, she seemed to consider her looks as quite insignificant.

"Here you go!" She slammed the drinks down on the table. "Say, did you hear this one?" and she proceeded to tell us the first of several jokes that always had us laughing despite the impropriety of many. If you were not given the full dose of Barbara's buffoonery, the evening would not be complete. Patrons craved her attention and competed for more time with her.

"What'll it be?" Barbara asked, leaning over the table.

"I don't know, Barbara. What do I want tonight?" Mom asked comfortably, as if she were in her own kitchen nook.

"How 'bout a garbage omelet?" Barbara offered, which was basically everything from the ice box to make the best omelet you ever put in your mouth.

"That sounds good, perfect, and with a house salad to start. Thanks."

The rest of us ordered our favorites: "Fried chicken livers for me with fried okra and green beans. And I want to start with a small cup of your chicken and rice soup."

"I'll have the fried catfish with the beets and a baked potato."

"And I want the steak sandwich—cooked rare—with green beans, a baked potato, and a house salad to start."

Barbara scuttled from our table on to others, calling each patron by name and refreshing drinks with the confidence of a dancer who knows the routine by heart. She remembered people's personal stories, their children's names, their job opportunities, and their challenges. She knew her food, so to speak, and folks trusted her implicitly. Most would get up from one of Barbara's tables shaking their heads muttering to themselves, "That Barbara is something else," and chuckling about the latest joke they could tell at the office the next day. Talk about an upper— she was better than a B12 shot or a session on the therapist's couch.

I don't know much about Barbara's journey. She is one of those invisible folks just doing her job as it intersects with our own routines. I knew she was married, divorced, and had a grown son. And like so many, Barbara made ends meet for her modest life through serving food in a local diner. I wonder if anyone aspires to wait tables twelve to fourteen hours a day in a small town for just above minimum wage. I don't know what Barbara's aspirations were as a young girl, nor do I know if she was living her dream. What I do know is that she was doing her job with an extraordinary, humorous energy and a funny form of grace. These made Barbara stand out.

If I were to ask Barbara what she had wanted to do when she grew up, she would likely have swatted that question off with disdain, as if it were a mosquito on a hot, humid night. At this stage in her life, she probably thought the answer irrelevant. She was doing what she needed to do and seasoning it with a little salt, pepper, and a dash of Tabasco. She was creating the right recipe for her life.

"Here you go. The steak sandwich, the livers, the catfish, and the omelet! Now, I'll be right back with some hot rolls. Anything else y'all need? Enjoy! Oh, and remind me to tell you the one I just heard—it's a goodie." And with that, she was off.

Spreading Magic Dust

I am certain Barbara left this world not realizing the lasting impression she left on so many. She bused tables and fixed cocktails while serving two types of soul food, one that fed our bodies and the other that fed our hearts. She became an extended member of many families. Though our visits were episodic in nature, the ritual of going to Mollie's and seeing Barbara, Paul, and Betty took on a familiar rhythm. The imprints made during our many evenings there are permanent.

I believe we make our own destiny by choosing to make the most of what we have been given. The greatest riches are those without material value, those that cannot be physically seen. We mine our treasures from within ourselves. Barbara may or may not have been consciously digging for her own riches, yet, like so many who cross our paths, she taught this lesson in the most humble of ways. Barbara found and brought pleasure through the simplest ways. She showed up. She was real. She had no false illusions. She simply did her job to the best of her ability and spread magic dust in the process.

One of the choices we are all given is the opportunity to lighten or to burden the moments for those around us. We can choose to create an aura of positive energy or of despair and gloom. When we leave a trail of brightness as we pass through others' lives, we leave the legacy of being remembered with a smile. Barbara and her jokes and her energy continued to draw my family back to Mollie's for the sparkle she served with the chicken livers.

Being Present in the Moment: Moving Toward Alignment

Questions to consider:

- From what source do you think Barbara drew her ability to serve love, laughter, and warmth?
- What is the "aura" you want others to remember about you?
- How can you lighten the load of others as you encounter them?

Do all the good you can, by all the means you can,
in all the ways you can, in all the places you can, at all the times
you can, to all the people you can, as long as ever you can.
—John Wesley

Changing the Frame, Loving the Moon

As I bustled through the Saint Louis airport, I was methodically structuring the next day's activities in my mind. I had a full day with new clients and wanted to exceed their expectations. The airport was surprisingly busy for 9:30 p.m. As I rounded the corner to baggage claim and ground transportation, I saw the most beautiful sight for any business traveler: my name clearly written on a sign held by an older man in a dark suit, tie, and cap.

"Hello, you Miss Kaufman? My name's Al. This all you have, or do you have luggage?"

"No, this is it. We're good to go."

"Well, don't you worry 'bout anything. I'll have you there in no time. We're about forty-five minutes away this time of night."

Al looked as if he were nearing or past retirement age. Dapper in style, carriage, and dress, he had a short clip to his step, keeping his own rhythm. Deliberate and focused, he loaded the trunk within seconds.

"Oh, my goodness, just look at that moon, would you?" I said. "Is that not simply gorgeous?"

"I love it. Loved it all night long."

"Where are you from? I hear a familiar accent."

"Oh, you won't know it. A small town in Arkansas. Ever heard of Proctor?"

"Why, yes! It's on the way to Memphis! I was raised in Hot Springs, and my sister lived in Memphis for a while."

"Goodness sakes! I never met anyone who ever heard of Proctor! Yep, I was raised there with my grandparents. A farmin' town."

"It's a small world. How long have you been driving?"

"Fifty-seven years, ever since I was eight years old on my granddad's farm. I had to sit on a stack of books just to see over the dash. I could just reach the pedals. It was an old stick shift. Learned to drive on the back dirt roads on the farm. All I ever done, 'cept for a job in a factory for a short time. Hated it. Drove long haul a while. Good money."

"Bet you've met a lot of folks."

That was like opening a canister of Pillsbury crescent rolls. Stories burst forth. He told me about famous and not-so-famous folks he had met over the years, interesting routes he had taken, fares he had been paid, and stimulating conversations he'd had. After almost a half hour with his hardly taking a breath, I wedged in a question.

"Al, you clearly love what you do. What do you think is the secret? I'm just curious because I meet folks all the time who are unhappy in their work. You must have issues with your work, too, like long hours, bad weather, delayed flights, and disgruntled clients. I know the folks I bump into along the way as I travel globally aren't always the most pleasant. How do you do it?"

With a huge guffaw, he replied, "Geez, never been asked that question before. I dunno. My grandmama always told me life is what you make it. Guess I took that one home with me. She said you gotta go to church, have faith, and work hard. Guess I ebb and flow on the first one. Church is not my long suit, so to speak, but I never lost my faith, and workin' hard is all I know. So all the other stuff is just 'static on the line,' as my grandson says. You just go with the flow. I've never been able to change no one, so I just keep smilin' and doin' my thing, and it rolls off. You know?"

"I think I get it, but how do you let go of the rude clients—you know, the ones who are really ugly?"

"That's like askin' me how I let go of death and taxes," he said, chuckling. "My line o' work is gonna always bring folks who are frustrated and just 'tired of it' across my path. I don't control them any more than I control death and taxes. So, you gotta make peace with 'em—just like with death and taxes."

"That's asking a lot considering how many hours you work and how many people you meet."

"Anyway, life's just too short to let folks ruin even one minute of my short time here. Gotta a few years left, and they gonna be lived the way I wanna. Gonna have fun with my grandchildren and my wife of over fifty years. I love meetin' folks. Try to shed a bit of light—then let it, and them, go. We all get ticked off from time to time. I'm just a driver, not the president, a CEO, or a scientist workin' on a cure for cancer. I just keep perspective, but what in the world do I know?"

As we rolled into the air force base where I was to lead a strategic session the following morning, that full moon was still bright, full, and high in the sky.

"Al, thanks so much. Just look at that moon. Perfect," I said as he unloaded my bags.

"You so welcome, Miss. Love that you love moons as much as me. Most never comment. Have a great day tomorrow. Knock 'em dead. And remember, life's short. Keep your perspective. See ya!"

Awake to Life

Al was "livin' his life," "lovin' the moon," holding onto his faith, and keeping his focus on what mattered to him. He would have appreciated a favorite book of my mom's, one I grew to respect on a deeper level as I grew older: *As a Man Thinketh* by James Allen.

"As a man thinketh in his heart, so is he," found in Proverbs 23:7, suggests that our attitudes play an enormous part in the successes or failures we experience in our lives. I often use the phrase, "Let's change the frame," when tackling an issue, resolving a personal dispute, or making sense of what appears to be an unjust decision. Changing the frame involves altering our perspective and attitude to view our experience through another set of lenses.

A friend of mine was laid off recently from his position at a nonprofit agency in Texas, due to budget cuts. After the initial shock, he was challenged to *change the frame* of the situation. He did this with grace, integrity, and strength by reaching out to every board member with handwritten notes thanking them for the opportunity to serve them and their joint cause. He was wise enough to believe that once he publicly declared this attitude and embraced the "high road," his internal perspective would change toward the positive. Rather than hosting a pity party, he chose a difficult yet powerful approach. Imagine the impact those handwritten letters had on those board members, perhaps changing the frame of their thinking about the difficult decisions they had made.

Al understands maintaining a positive perspective. His philosophy is to keep things simple. He looks at the moon and sees the beauty and magnitude of the world. He embraces the entire experience of life. He sincerely engages with his passengers, making their trips pleasant and smooth. He appears to have "reframing" all figured out. He has perspective about what really matters to him. He has effectively aligned his values, his vocation, and his focus, enhancing his own life and the lives of those with whom he comes in contact.

I am grateful to Al for that moonlit ride. He reminded me once again how important interacting with the folks who brush up against us in our lives in incidental meetings can be. Often, we never know their names, yet if we are awake to our brief glimpse into their lives, we may be like Al who lives in the moment, maintains his perspective, and treats each of his passengers as someone special. He also reminded me how each day we can choose to find pleasure in simple things: the full moon on a clear summer night, a mockingbird's song in the early morning hours, or the smell of freshly mown grass. These are the sensory gifts of everyday life, if we are present and awake enough to enjoy them. Al certainly does.

James Allen believes "a man is literally what he thinks, his character being the complete sum of all his thoughts. The more tranquil a man becomes, the greater is his success, his influence, his power for good. Calmness of mind is one of the beautiful jewels of wisdom. The circumstances do not make the man, they reveal him." Al would, no doubt, agree.

Being Present in the Moment:
Moving toward Alignment

Questions to consider:

- Can you recall a situation in your life when you decided to "change the frame" and found that the circumstances became more positive? What did you observe and learn from that experience?
- Have you been too preoccupied to "be present in the moment" and missed an opportunity to gain insight?
- Do you have a single phrase that captures your most frequent attitude, your "frame"? How does this phrase serve you?

A great attitude does much more than turn on the lights in our worlds; it seems to magically connect us to all sorts of serendipitous opportunities that were somehow absent before the change.
—Earl Nightingale

Undivided Attention

"Here now, come put your feet in this warm water. There, there—comfy? Can I get you something to drink?" she asked as I slowly slid into the already-vibrating massage chair.

"Oh, that would be nice. A bottle of cold water, please."

"Be right back. Just relax," she whispered, echoing the soothing tone of the spa.

Bonnie's heavy-set frame was cloaked in a dull lavender dress hanging loosely from her shoulders, softly framing her coffee-colored skin. Peeking out from under the long skirt were murky tan support hose that bunched up where they squeezed into her black lace-up orthopedic shoes. As she walked away, her staunch bearing rocked back and forth, dipping from each shoulder.

I felt myself slipping into a state somewhere between REM sleep and Zen meditation. The stresses of the day gradually slipped into the water, and I settled into what I hoped would be an hour of pure sensory pleasure and relaxation. I had known Bonnie for just a few months as I was traveling from out of town and would see her only infrequently. She had been highly recommended. Her leg massages were deeply invigorating, and she had a strong and often controlling way that gave assurance that she knew what she was doing. As a manicurist and pedicurist for more than forty-five years, she certainly did.

Bonnie's story was one I admired, and yet one I feel certain is not unique. Bonnie was raising her six grandchildren, ages seven to seventeen, due to her daughter's incarceration for several years. Bonnie had been married to her husband for more than forty-five years. He worked in a nearby warehouse as a supervisor, had been with the same company for almost thirty years, and was nearing retirement.

Bonnie gave anywhere between eight and ten pedicures a day, six days a week. I was her last appointment this Friday afternoon, so I imagined she would be quite exhausted.

"Thanks, Bonnie," I said as she handed me the ice-cold bottle of Evian. "How are you today?"

"Oh, I am just dandy. And how are you, Miss Kristin?"

"I am OK. Boy, it has been a tough week. Lots of pressure. We have a huge quota, and I am just not sure we are going to make it."

"Hmm. Tell me more."

This was Bonnie's specialty. She would create a physical environment of total tranquility and then invite you to disrupt the peaceful waters with your own personal monsoon of worries. She would sit there hours upon hours, massaging feet and calves, trimming cuticles, and listening to long lamentations with the patience of Job. That particularly day, I must have gone on for half an hour, barely coming up for breath, with Bonnie adding a "hmmm" or "I see" or offering well-timed insightful clichés. She was pummeling, kneading, and buffing with the fervor of a baker rolling out a fresh pan of biscuits, not showing even the slightest hint of weariness.

Finally, feeling a bit guilty for dumping my heavy load squarely onto her shoulders, I offered: "Bonnie, forgive me. I have gone on and on about me. Please tell me about you and your week! What do you have planned for this weekend?"

"Oh, hon. My weeks just keep on going and going. It has been a good week."

Trying to mimic her tactic, I asked, "How so?"

"I have been real busy. I've done eight or nine services each day since Monday, and I'm coming in again tomorrow as I have clients who want to see me. Can't complain. I'm busy. Saving for Christmas. My husband and I want a nice Christmas for the children."

"Wow, Bonnie. It's only July. You are planning ahead."

"Got to. Have sports uniforms, Boy Scout dues, and other school supplies to pay for. We take the few extra dollars left each month and put them in our Christmas fund."

Humbled and inspired by her discipline and encouraged by her openness, I inquired further. "You know, Bonnie, for the brief time I have known you, you always seem so 'up.' Given the challenges of raising your precious grandchildren at this stage in your life, how in the world do you do it?"

"Gosh, Miss Kristin. This ain't nothing. You do what you gotta do. I can either do it with a smile or a scowl. We love our grandchildren, and we are fortunate to be able to do what we do. They are blessings, you know."

"I know, Bonnie, but what keeps you going?! I mean, *really*, Bonnie!"

"Now, now," she calmly continued, "my momma used to always tell me when you think you got it worse than everybody else, put your sights on the other person. There is nothing that cures feeling sorry for yourself better than thinking about

Kristin S. Kaufman

someone else and giving someone your undivided attention. It takes the focus off of you.

"So, that's one reason I love giving manicures and pedicures every day. I get to listen to stories in folks' lives, help lighten their loads, and give them a small dose of pleasure in their hectic days. I give them undivided attention—and I bet in some cases, that is the first time they have had undivided attention all week. That just gives me energy. Makes me feel good."

"You know, Bonnie, you're right about giving folks your undivided attention. So often these days, we compete with TV, cell phones, and Blackberries when we are talking or meeting with someone. Even though you are working so diligently on my feet and legs, you are really present and fully attuned to what I am saying. I feel that. Thank you for listening to me all these past weeks."

As Bonnie finished the treatment that day, she continued to offer her perspectives on my travails and challenges. As if Bonnie had not given enough, as I was leaving, she quietly came up to me and whispered: "Psalm 91:2—'He is my refuge and my fortress,'" gave me a hug, and wished me a nice weekend. I rushed home to read this verse, and I knew where Bonnie derived her strength.

Refuge in the Present

Through her life, Bonnie reminded me that one of the greatest gifts we give another person is our undivided attention. So often we are distracted when we are with other people. Distractions can come in a myriad of forms: cell phones, television, thinking of what we are going to say when they are finished, scanning the room to see who else is present at an important meeting, or simply not being fully present in the moment with that person.

There is nothing more powerful than feeling and knowing that someone is totally "into you" and to what you are saying; yet so often we let the sunshine of those moments get clouded by our own narcissism and preoccupations. Bonnie's life exemplifies pure and selfless interest in the other person and sets an inspiring example to follow.

Psalm 91:2 says, "He is my refuge and my fortress, my God, in him I will trust." Bonnie had a centered stalwart resolve that anyone who met her would have known. She was also totally aligned to her strengths, her gifts and talents, and the loves of her life—her family. She knew who she was, what her purpose was to be, how she could contribute to her family, her clients, and throughout her life. She lived openly and authentically, and she anchored her authenticity through alignment to a higher power.

Bonnie lived a simple life. She quietly served her clients over the better half of her life, with many probably not even knowing her last name. Her faithful resolve and the unwavering attention to others resembled a mature, strong oak tree spreading her branches to offer shade to anyone who came into her presence. Our acknowledgment of her may be cursory and fleeting, but her presence is undeniable.

Being Present in the Moment:
Moving Toward Alignment

Questions to consider:

- • What holds you back from offering your undivided attention to others? What do you have to lose? What do you have to gain?
- • What lessons can you take away from Bonnie's life and replicate in your own?
- • What helped Bonnie stay aligned in her life? What anchors your life?

For it is in giving, that we receive.
—Saint Francis of Assisi

The
Moments
of Our Lives

The fist fight in my mind was between what I thought I should do and what I really wanted to do. Until then, most of my volunteer hours had been sorting clothes for resale, driving nails in a house for Habitat for Humanity, or boxing cans of food at the food bank. I really wanted a hands-on experience in a hospital, I thought.

The person in charge was a heavy-set, middle-aged woman with a face as unflinching as a cement wall. A cross between General Patton and Jane Hathaway from *The Beverly Hillbillies*, she was strong, officious, and organized. Her name was Billie. Billie chose to work here permanently because she had been a guest here at the facility for many years. Her own story is one of triumph.

I learned that Randy, her twelve-year-old son, had been mowing the backyard and spilled gasoline on his hands and legs. He went inside to wash it off, and fumes from an exposed gas heater caught him on fire. Burned on over 70 percent of his body, he braved more than twenty skin graft surgeries and painful treatments for more than eight years. Billie maintained that her work was her way of giving back and supporting other families facing the same challenges. Cement walls suddenly seemed strangely angelic.

Billie welcomed me, signed me in, and gave me my marching orders. I had already taken my TB test and passed all the other required clearances, so I was ready to work. My first duty was to sort little bottles of shampoo, soap, and other toiletries in sacks for the visiting families' rooms. Ironically, those first months I sought refuge in that back closet away from emotion, sadness, visible signs of illness, and death. The glimpses of sick children and grieving families had made me faint with feelings I wasn't sure I wanted to face. Burying myself in the business of bottles, I thought I could avoid getting too involved and just stay on the fringes.

"Hi," came a small perky voice from the couch in the lobby. I sighed. I was leaving for the day, and this intrusion thwarted my quick getaway. When I looked up, I caught a gasp mid-throat.

Sitting on a faded, putrid pink sofa was a waif of a person. Her small figure was a clothed skeleton with pointy bones lending shape to her blouse and capri pants. She had a loose bandage of gauze wrapped around her head. Around the base of her neck were short stubs of blond hair poking from the white turban. Half her face was covered by a stained bandage with an egg-shaped stuffing in place of her left eye. From a fragmented nose protruded a tube with a slow sludge of fluid trickling through to a bag fastened to her chest. The final frame to this image was a lopsided, gap-toothed smile, like a child waiting for the tooth fairy.

"Oh, hi. How are you today?" I said, gathering my composure and feeling the sting of guilt for wanting to leave early.

"I am doing great. I am out of the hospital today, and we get to go home tomorrow! I can't wait. My mom is in our room packing. I have cancer. I had an operation a few weeks ago to get rid of this tumor. The doctor said we could go home for a while. We've been here for several weeks. I'm so excited to see my little brother and my daddy. They are at home waiting for us," she said in an energetic flood, eager to share happy news.

"Where is home?" I asked, feeling a bit sick to my stomach.

"Waxahachie. My name is Kristen, by the way. What's yours?"

"No way! That is my name, too! Wow, that rarely happens. How do you spell yours?"

"K-r-i-s-t-e-n."

"Oh, mine is spelled K-r-i-s-t-i-n. You know, most girls my age spell theirs this way because there was a book that was very popular, *Kristin Lavernsdatter*, written by a Danish author, Sigrid Undset."

"Really? How cool. I haven't read it. I was named after a friend of my mom. She liked the name," she said, shrugging her shoulders.

We visited for a few more minutes, primarily about what Kristen wanted to do when she got home, what she was going to get to eat, and when she would go back to school. Gathering my things to leave, I told her I hoped to see her again and wished her a speedy recovery.

Several weeks passed, and I was visiting with Billie before I began my standard duties, when a small slumped image was wheeled through the doors and down the hallway to the special guest room wing.

"Billie, who was that? I don't believe I recognized him."

"That was Kristen. She was released from the hospital earlier today, and they will be leaving tomorrow to go home."

"What? I thought she had been released a month or two ago. That didn't even look like her. How is she?"

"You know we can't discuss the specifics. It's so sad. She is only twelve years old. You can go visit her if you would like. We won't need you up here in the front for a while."

Reluctantly, I headed to the wing reserved for those needing special protection from infection. I knocked on her door.

"Come in."

As I came through the door, I was greeted with a warm, weathered smile, "Hi. I'm Heather, Kristen's mom."

"I am Kristin, too. I came to see Kristen number one."

"How nice," she said, smiling quietly at my attempt at humor. "I know about you. Kristen, look who's here to see you."

As Kristen turned her wheelchair to face me, I felt as if I had gotten up too fast and saw fuzzy white specks. I steadied myself by placing my fingers on the bedside table. The entire left side of Kristen's head was gone. In its place were soft tissue and loose gauze covering what looked like a half-slanted triangle where a round circle once was. Her mouth and chin had been reduced to a small crevice through which she could breathe and sip nourishment, but her right eye was still blinking and bright blue.

"Hi, Kristin," she mumbled. "I'm glad to see you. I remember you. You have my name."

"I'm glad to see you, too."

"We're going home tomorrow. I probably won't see you again. The doctor said that I won't have any more surgeries because the tumor is still growing and is too big. So Mommy is taking me home to be with my brother and daddy before I go to heaven."

As I stood there listening to this matter-of-fact death description from this twelve-year-old, I felt hollow. Her mother was standing there with her hands clasped in front of her, a proud but sad stoic mask on her face.

I stammered, hoping for something wise or comforting to

say, and, failing at both, squeaked out, "I am so sorry, Kristen. I don't know what to say, other than I am so glad to have met you, and I am sorry I won't get to know you better."

She reached out, took my right hand and pulled me to her. The whiff of medicine and raw flesh was almost too much as I was enveloped by all sixty-five pounds of her. She tightened her grip on me and whispered, "Thanks for being so nice to me." I returned the hug with as much strength as I could muster. As I left, I clasped hands with her mom and gave her what I hoped was a reassuring smile, told her I would keep them in my prayers, and left the room.

I walked back to the front desk with full eyes and heart, realizing the timing for my meeting Kristen was divine in nature. It changed my life.

The Angels Among Us

My mom always taught me that we never know what we are going to do or say that may impact another. Kristen's quiet acceptance of a diseased, short life impacted my perspective on time. Guilt and responsibility may have initiated this experience; love and desire quickly took their place. Kristen's life changed mine and became a catalyst in my growing appreciation of time. We do not control time. It always runs out. If we are wise, we make time now for those things that are important to us.

The moments and the people in our lives are the two most critical components in experiencing fulfillment in life, personally and professionally. As individuals living in transformational times, we spend our moments doing things that help us grow, stretch, evolve, and contribute. We know this, yet we often struggle with how to identify what is most important, how to prioritize, and how to keep those most valued responsibilities sacred.

Other voices, real or imagined, can influence our ordering of priorities. We need to listen to our own voice. Had I not listened to an inner voice beckoning me to Kristen, I would have missed a gift that continues to reverberate in my life.

The singular moment is really all we have, yet many of us put our life on hold—waiting for "something" or "someone" to enter when "real life" will begin. Whatever we are doing at this moment—reading this book, drinking coffee, multitasking, getting through e-mail—is the gift. The mundane moments go by so fast and so routinely that we often forget that they add up to our life. Each moment is unequivocally a gift. The next is not guaranteed.

Some do not fully comprehend until the moments are few, death is within sight, and they are "on the edge." The moments become more potent, more precious, a treasured commodity. What are we waiting for? Why not live each and every day as if it were our last? Every single moment is a gift—to be present, to live, to think, to taste, to see, to smell, to feel, and to contribute. When we get out of alignment with the present moment, we miss out on life.

What would happen if we had just one centered conversation at a time? What would happen if we turned off the cell phones when visiting with another person? What could happen if, instead of making the act of "going for the close" or "negotiating the deal" our primary intention, we focused on being truly present with the person with whom we are meeting? What possibilities could emerge? By being in alignment with what is happening, when it is happening, we open up our greatest opportunities for growth and learning. Our thoughts, decisions, and actions will be powered by what we experience when we are experiencing them. These are the moments called "Life."

Kristen realized her moments were few. She wanted to spend those remaining with family she loved. My experience with Kristen reminded me that we can choose to be present in each moment of our lives, purposely and intentionally.

Being Present in the Moment: Moving Toward Alignment

Questions to consider:

- What are you doing to make each moment of your life all that it can be?
- What gifts did Kristen and Kristin exchange during their brief friendship? What did one teach? What did one learn?
- In your life, do you seek out the less visible people to learn their stories and share yours?

The whole of life, from the moment you are
born to the moment you die, is a process of learning.
—Jiddu Krishnamurti

A Funny Valentine

As I drove my rented blue Camaro convertible through the scenic landscape from San Francisco to Carmel, I was on a high, having recently accepted a new position at my company. I was meeting a friend for a weekend at the fabulous Highlands Inn in Carmel/Monterey. When I reached the resort, the cancellation message on my voicemail told me I would be dining alone on Friday evening of Valentine's Day weekend. My disappointment gradually shifted to a strange sort of freedom.

Later, as the *maitre d'* seated me in the resort restaurant, I canvassed the room to see if there were any other solo diners. I was the only one, so I confidently smiled at the other couples in the room. This was going to be an evening to forget.

The dining room was arranged so that everyone had a pedestal on which to perch, which made teetering "on high" alone less than comfortable. Determined to enjoy my evening, I focused intently on the menu and wine list.

"Good evening. Dining alone?" asked the waiter, a tall muscular man with a beautiful olive complexion.

"Yes. Thank you."

"What may I bring you to drink? A glass of champagne, martini, glass of wine? What is your pleasure?" At this point, all I was thinking was that alcohol in any form would do just fine.

"A nice glass of champagne sounds lovely."

"Perfect choice. I will be right back," he said from the back of his throat, as he all but clicked his heels together and nodded in acknowledgment.

"So happy to have your approval," I muttered to myself. I looked up to see an older couple smiling at me from a few tables away. I smiled back, and the woman nodded her head, while the gentleman raised his glass and mouthed "Cheers." I smiled and raised my water glass. This small gesture began the first rhythmic stanza of pantomime between us.

My evening meal was a culinary *Madame Butterfly*. The combinations of flavors and textures were powerful, stirring mouthwatering delight in every bite. I laced each melt-in-your-mouth morsel with a luscious Cakebread Cellars Chardonnay.

At the onset of each course, my across-the-room friends would lift their glasses to me as I would do the same to them. We would nod politely, smile, and mouth "yummy" or "divine" at each savory experience. Before I could ask for my check, the woman leaned forward and whispered loudly in my direction: "What an evening! Did you enjoy dinner?"

"Yes, very much. How could I not?"

"We know this may seem a bit forward, but you seem like such a charming young woman. We were wondering if you would like to join us for an after-dinner drink? We enjoy grappa or Sambuca after our meals. We would love for you to join us."

Warmed by their friendly gestures all evening, and not wanting to go back to my bungalow, I answered without hesitation, "I would be delighted. Thank you."

They unfolded like praying mantises as they emerged from their table. Both were much taller than they appeared at the table and must have been in their late seventies. The gentleman, white-haired and distinguished, carried an expensive, ivory-inlaid cane with a silver end and wore a dark suit complete with matching yellow Hermes tie and pocket square. He gallantly reached over to pull out her chair so she could move more easily and extended his hand to her.

"Come, dear. Let's go the bar," he said to her. "My name is John, and this is Irene."

She had dyed blonde hair tied into a tall bouffant bun. She was liberal in her application of makeup and reminded me of someone who had once been in Vaudeville: dark raccoon eyes, bright red cheeks, and lipstick that extended far beyond her lips. She wore a floating dress in a feminine floral print, clearly designed to create a svelte mirage. When she moved, lavender filled the air.

As we meandered across the hall to the bar, I introduced myself and shared what brought me to California. We entered the dark paneled room with a fireplace burning at the opposite end, where a five-piece jazz combo played quiet renditions of Tommy Dorsey, Glenn Miller, and a few Frank Sinatra tunes.

"Let's sit at the bar," John said. "That's where all the action is."

Giggling to myself, lost in my image of what "action" meant to him, I snuggled into the leather barstool and swiveled to face John and Irene. I learned that he had been a developer of properties around the United States. He was a widower who had lost his wife several years before; and Irene was a widow who had lost her husband more than a decade before. As couples, they had been friends for more than thirty-five years. Irene was the singer in a club that John had developed over forty years ago. She had a tremendous career traveling with bands around the country and finally became a permanent fixture in a famous nightclub in California.

They reminisced about their lives, their marriages, and their longstanding friendship. Each year, on Valentine's Day, they had a standing date since they both lost their partners. They were clearly devoted to one another and shared a uniquely interlocked past.

As the evening grew long, I said, "Your lives have been so rich and full. Thank you for sharing them with me."

Irene got out of her chair and slowly made her way up to the stage. She whispered something to the pianist and then took the microphone from its stand. I had thought all night how fabulous it would have been to have heard her sing.

"Good evening. If you would indulge me, I would like to offer a song this evening, a favorite of mine by Rodgers and Hart. I want to dedicate this to my new little friend at the bar, who has graced us with her interest and youthful enthusiasm. She is my 'Funny Valentine.'"

Irene began to sing in a gravelly, deep alto voice, as she must have done a hundred times. I reached over and touched John's arm, and he put his hand on my hand. He whispered, "She never does this. You clearly must have touched her heart."

We sat there and listened to Irene: "My funny valentine, sweet comic valentine, you make me smile with my heart. . . ."

As the evening came to a close, three strangers who shared an unexpected bond gave each other tender hugs and said good-bye. All odds told us this evening was to be our only meeting in life. What a lovely evening it was.

Dinner with a Side Dish of Sharing

Love can descend upon our lives as quietly as a butterfly lighting on an arm. I never dreamed Irene and John would enter my life that night. Nor had I expected the lasting memory I would carry from our shared experience. How many times do we turn a deaf ear or blind eye to these strangers who breeze in and out of our lives? What opportunities do we let pass because we are not paying attention?

Life and business are truly about building relationships, perhaps initiated through incidental meetings such as mine with Irene and John that serendipitous evening. My parents have always maintained that the keys to business and life are the relationships. I was raised with the perspective that life is "all about people." It is not about collecting hundreds of cards and having empty conversations at the myriad of networking events that proliferate today. This kind of networking is vapid, shallow, and insincere if only on a surface level.

Building relationships is the antithesis; it creates fertile ground for the seeds of connection we mutually plant to grow. Irene and John were not seeking a profitable meeting. They reached out to me from an authentic desire to get to know me.

The litmus test for sincere and genuine conversations and relationships is to ask ourselves, "Who or what does this serve?" If the answer is "me and me alone," the relationship will be short-lived. Irene and John gave of their precious time together and briefly shared their lives with me. They wanted to include me in their evening so that I would not be alone on Valentine's Day weekend. By being gracious to me that evening, they enjoyed a rich, fulfilling experience. By being open in heart and spirit, they reminded me how we can create a flow of energy, which ultimately will come back to us and enrich the lives of those we meet.

The evening I met John and Irene, I believed I was the only person in the room on whom they were focused. When we meet others, nothing is more powerful than feeling as if the person is totally, 100 percent focused on *you*, listening intently to your spoken and unspoken words. Then you are present in the moment with that person.

Being present in the moment is indeed "where the juice is." We have all been in the situation at a party, a networking function, and even an intimate dinner party, when the person with whom we are visiting is surveying the room to see who else is there, who the next "contact" needs to be. What a missed opportunity. Having these complete strangers envelop me with love, genuine interest, and attention was refreshing, unexpected, and lasting. Irene and John approached life with an abundant attitude. They lived life large, and they were generous.

Over the years I have been amazed to watch the correlation between the wildly successful individuals and the marginally successful. The most successful are those who have been unconditionally generous with their time, business relationships, and knowledge. They are secure in their philosophy based on abundance, not scarcity, and share openly. Those who hoard their time, their knowledge, and even their experiences come from a scarcity mentality and create that reality for themselves. I have no doubt that Irene and John lived an abundant life because they gave abundantly.

Irene and John created a magical evening for me. I wonder what led them to reach out to me. I wonder if someone had reached out to them earlier in their lives that left a similar impression. Whatever led them to extend their hands and hearts that evening launched an expression of love whose first chorus was "My Funny Valentine."

Being Present in the Moment: Moving Toward Alignment

Questions to consider:

- Are you living with an open heart like Irene and John? What holds you back?
- When you meet a new person, are you focused on you or on how you might enrich that person's life?
- What gifts might you give and receive if you allow yourself to become vulnerable to spontaneous encounters?

Nothing is accidental in the universe.
—Joyce Carol Oates

Mon Plaisir

*B*ienvenue *chez nous, madame.* It is a beautiful night. May I bring you a glass of Bordeaux, Château Pichon-Longueville-Baron Pauillac, or maybe you prefer a burgundy, a Louis Jadot, perhaps?"

Instantly charmed as only a warm French accent espousing expensive wine can do, I answered, "*Oui,* the Bordeaux. *Merci beaucoup.*"

"*Parfait!* I will be right back."

As I nestled into my favorite French bistro in London, I surveyed the quaint, familiar room. The narrow space fit no more than twenty small tables placed closely together. Each was neatly wrapped in crisp white linens christened with a single votive candle. The walls were graced with a nostalgic hodgepodge of old photographs, mirrors, and family memorabilia, as the restaurant had been in the same family for many years. I had taken the only open table in a far corner and had a perfect spot to watch humanity. Spirits coupled with the dimly lit ambiance gave couples permission to embrace passion and persuasiveness with equal aplomb. The energy was Parisian *amour* at its finest.

"*Voila!*" he enthusiastically boasted as the glass of crimson nectar magically appeared in front of me. Startled from my romantic musing, I looked up to see this was not my waiter but the owner of the establishment.

"*Madame,* you have been here many times before. Welcome back, I am happy to see you again. What may I bring you tonight, or do you prefer to take your time and linger with us a while?"

"Yes, thank you. I have had a very busy day in the city and want to relax a while, and just disappear."

"*Oui, oui.* You have busy career? You are American, no? Yet, you are here often."

Enchanted by his interest, I began to tell an abbreviated version of my story. He hung on every word. He inquired about what led me to my profession, what kept me hooked to the global pace and travel. He even displayed interest in my personal life.

Remarkably, despite my wanting to disappear earlier, I found myself fully engaged in the conversation and invited him to join me at my table. This was the beginning of an enlightening evening.

His name was Gilles. His *joie de vivre* was contagious. Though his voice was deep, it had an upward tilt like an audible curly cue. His snicker of a laugh shook every whisker in his mustache as he would snort with abandon. Happily married for more than thirty years, he and his wife had two grown children and one grandchild. Gilles had grown up in a small town just north of Paris, where his family owned the village delicatessen and small café, which served country French food to the locals. He had moved to London after he graduated from university and entered the investment banking industry.

Modestly, Gilles shared that he had experienced tremendous financial success early in his career through a combination of smart, shrewd moves coupled with a thriving economy.

"Gilles, how fortunate you are to have achieved financial security early in your life, giving you the freedom to pursue what you really wanted to do."

"No, no. You speak too soon. Let me tell you. I had achieved a great deal, you are right, yet I was not so fortunate. I made big mistakes. What could have been my 'nest egg,' to use an American term, I lost. My bad decision caused me to lose almost everything. Almost everything."

He paused, looked out over the street, and then continued.

"I was destitute. My wife and I found ourselves with only a small amount left. Maria—that is my wife's name—had been a mom at home since we had married and had children and did not have any real professional skills. I was solely responsible not only for what had happened but also for what I had to do to fix it. That was a very dark time. Very dark."

Gilles' demeanor altered. His face appeared a pale gray, and the glint in his eyes and lilt in his voice were instantly gone.

"I am so sorry that happened. But look at where you are now. How in the world did you find yourself here?"

"*Oui. Oui.* This is the real story. To be truthful, I loved the financial business. Unlike what many may think, I didn't leave the financial business because I didn't like what I was doing. I actually did. When we lost all we had, my wife held the belief that everything happens for a reason. That may sound strange to you. As distraught as we were, she encouraged me to look at this experience with curiosity. So I began to discover what I really wanted in life. Money is still important and a reality, believe me; I do not want to romanticize.

"Yet I think I was given a chance to take a breath and really try to uncover what I really wanted to do—above and beyond just being a husband and father. I guess I naively thought if I could tap into that, the rest would fall into place. That horrible situation actually opened the door for me to explore what that might be. In some ways it gave me permission. I spent almost a year mulling about and trying to get in touch with what I was really passionate about. You know, what makes me happy to my core. I was still working in the financial business, but I allowed myself to consider other things.

"I don't know what I would have done without Maria," he said, shaking his head back and forth. "She was a rock. We had only a little of our savings left, and three young children. In some ways, I was just going through the motions in my job. It was a scary time. We would not be here were it not for her."

Spellbound and touched by his vulnerability, I asked, "How did you finally come to realize opening a bistro was what you wanted to do? What a change from investment banking."

"*Oui*. When I finally let go of what I thought I was *supposed* to do, which was something I think I just fell into while I was at university, and opened up to what I really wanted to do, the choice was natural. I've loved the food business my whole life. It's my passion. Mama and Papa had raised me and my sisters in it. They always said they were in the business of spreading love, and food was just one way. It just felt right.

"People have asked me if I was scared, and the answer is a giant *oui!* At that point I thought I didn't have that much more to lose; I had already lost so much. The shackles were gone, so to speak. I took the plunge, and thankfully it turned out all right. *Merveilleux!*"

I smiled broadly and raised my glass. "Congratulations. I'm so happy for you, your family, and your life. Thank you so much for sharing your story with me."

"*Merci. Merci.* I know that, had I not lost what I did so many years ago, I might still be in that industry today. That wouldn't have been awful, but the loss was actually a catalyst for me to rethink how I really wanted to live my life. It gave me a chance to figure that out.

"The change hasn't been easy. It takes a lot of hard work and discipline to make it in the food business. But I knew this was what I truly wanted. I'm passionate about what we do and about the clientele we serve. I knew, with the love of my family, we could build a good business. And I know what I do brings joy to my life because I am in the business of serving and bringing love and joy to others. Does it get any better than that? After almost twenty years, I am in bliss."

Mon Plaisir . . . My Pleasure

That evening decades ago in London remains one of my most special evenings. Gilles had the courage to weather a challenging situation, look deep within himself, and follow his passion. It resonates with me still.

Our quest for alignment, of integrating our gifts and talents with our purpose, begins with getting to know ourselves. Gilles's deliberate journey toward greater self-awareness came through hardship, as so many of our greatest lessons and epiphanies do. An old Chinese proverb states: "My barn having burned to the ground, I can now see the moon." He had a choice to see life differently given the forced freedom to do so.

Hearing Gilles recount his realization of when the "story" he had embraced in college no longer represented what he felt or what he believed was compelling. We often keep playing and listening to the stories we have recorded on our soul's stereos even when they no longer represent our authenticity, if they ever did. This continuum of "shoulds" and "oughts" and ongoing comparisons to others' career choices, professions, expectations, responsibilities, and status in life do not serve us well. Only when we realize those stories are no longer our stories can we choose to write our own new chapter.

Gilles tapped into what really made his heart sing. He realized his love and passion for creating a warm, inviting establishment to serve food and drink to his clientele was what resonated in his soul. He then embarked upon this newly discovered vision with hard work, discipline, and intensity. I am quite certain Gilles had moments of doubt, fear, and concern for the unknown and what could happen.

What inspired me was that despite having made poor judgments in the past where he literally lost almost all of his financial security, he had the courage to risk it all again to follow his passion. This grit, this ability to embrace fear, was a catalyst for Gilles. He focused on his "end game," his goal, and powered through what I can only imagine were often scary times.

I have been told many times that fear rises up when we are on the right course and that not feeling stretched, challenged, and often scared means that the task, goal, or dream we are pursuing is not big enough. What a paradox, albeit a reassuring one. Out of Gilles's prior misfortune came an opportunity to fly and to transform his life.

One of the most compelling threads of Gilles's story is the pervasiveness of love. Gilles openly shared his love and devotion for his wife, Maria. He spoke reverently and with much appreciation of his parents, how they raised him and his sisters with an emphasis on spreading love and joy among their village patrons. Love was a value that ultimately fed, and also drove, his choices in life and ultimately in his profession. His restaurant business is nurtured by his joy in "spreading love through food," and doing so brings him joy. Gilles loves his work, and it will be the gift that he keeps on giving, creating a wonderful cycle of self-renewal and fulfillment when his passions, fueled by love, are in alignment with purpose.

How grateful I am for these moments when a stranger opened his heart and story with me. This incidental encounter was one of many that have served me on my own road to alignment and have helped to reveal my own bliss. Meeting Gilles was a gift and *mon plaisir.*

Being Present in the Moment:
Moving Toward Alignment

Questions to consider:

- What stories are you allowing to play in your mind that may not reflect your true purpose? What do you know in your heart to be true yet are afraid to acknowledge because of the action this may require?
- What are you willing to risk to follow your dream? What have you become more aware of because of hardships and losses in your life?
- How is love interwoven in your life? How do you let love manifest in your work and workplace?

What the caterpillar calls the end of the world, the master calls a butterfly.
—Richard Bach

Every Day a Celebration

It is funny how seemingly insignificant seconds can turn into life-framing moments. My father was having a birthday, and my sister and I had come home to Hot Springs to celebrate. As a family, we seldom if ever miss celebrating our birthdays together—eighty-two is a milestone by anyone's standards. We were planning a quiet meal at our favorite Italian restaurant downtown.

Our hometown has always been a tourist destination, from the days of Al Capone and Owney Madden to thoroughbred racing and simulcasting. More recently, the Harley Davidson crowd has found it to be a perfect collection of hills, wide open spaces, and nearby mountains. This particular weekend the town was full of baby boomer rebels flexing their metallic muffler muscles up and down Central Avenue.

Concerned about parking, always at a premium when the bikers come to town, we arranged for a taxi.

"Good evening. How are you?" My father greeted the taxi driver as my mom, sister, and I crawled into the back seat.

"I'm just fine! Where are you heading tonight?" asked the driver, perfectly groomed and very accommodating to my father, who was struggling to bend his eighty-two-year-old body into the seat.

"We're going to Belle Arte, please."

"My name is Damian. What's the celebration tonight?"

"It's my birthday, and my girls are in town. Every day is a celebration, you know, when you hit my age."

"That's nice. You're lucky, you know. I drove a woman to Louisiana earlier this week. She came to town because her relative died and they had the services and the reading of the will. She didn't get anything and her relatives didn't even offer to take her back home. So she hired me to drive her four hundred miles. Just got back this morning. "

"You mean you drove her all the way back to Louisiana? In a taxi?"

"Yep. The whole way. She was really upset. I bet she was seventy or eighty years old. I think she was partly mad and partly hurt. She hardly spoke to me the whole way to Louisiana. Can you imagine having to take a taxi across state lines to get home?"

"No," we said in unison.

"That is so sad," I whispered to my mom. "What in the world must have happened in that family?"

"From what I put together," Damian chimed in, overhearing what I had said, "they had a huge fight about money, apparently before this guy died. The family was just getting back at her. It was ugly, from what I figure."

"What does a taxi ride to Louisiana cost?" I asked, forgetting my southern manners forbidding the discussions of money and price.

"She paid me three hundred bucks. No tip."

"No tip? What do you mean, no tip?" I asked, incredulous that a four-hundred-mile trip didn't warrant a tip of any sort.

"Well, she didn't have any money. Three hundred bucks was it. I felt sorry for her."

We just sat there lost in our own thoughts. What was there to say? Here was a man, perhaps struggling with his own financial worries, yet his compassion for this woman was clear.

"I hate to think that lady went home with no family connection. Lost 'em—all because of some battle over money. Don't they realize that all we have is our family, our friends, and love? You know, like this birthday you're celebrating. My family doesn't have much money or a fancy house, but we sure do have fun together. I've got a little girl, and we love her so much. Of course I hope to get her things I never had, but I don't ever want money or greed to come between me and my folks. I am just so grateful we have each other. "

We pulled up to our destination. Damian turned around to face us as we unbuckled our seat belts and opened our doors.

"I hope y'all have a great time tonight. Man, you are lucky," he said to my father.

"Yes, I am. We don't really have to look that far to realize that, do we, Damian? Thanks again. Good luck to you!"

As we meandered down the sidewalk to celebrate my father's birthday, we knew we were grateful for so much more.

Gratitude for Blessings Great and Small

Blessings were the focus of that evening, for us and for our driver. As Damian pointed out, not all of us have our health, wealth, or prosperity, and in many cases, not even a loving family. In times of greatest celebration, we quickly recognize our blessings, yet in the day-to-day struggles of life we often lose sight of what each of us has to be grateful for. Meeting Damian, with his uncomplicated perspective, served as a reminder.

Damian's story of the elderly woman reminded me that what we have is right now—nothing else. Her life changed in an instant. I wondered what she thought about on the way back to Louisiana. Would her choices on how she spends her remaining moments be different?

That evening, like all evenings with my family, was full of love. Each one of us has the ability to give love every day. This love may take many forms: whether rescuing a puppy and taking it into our home, bailing out a stranger whose house is being foreclosed, or driving a woman four hundred miles because her situation was sad. We see this sort of "love" daily, if we keep our eyes open. Love is the glue that binds all our collective experiences and becomes the light illuminating the way to our own sense of individual alignment.

We also have the gift of the lessons we learn every day. We rarely recognize these experiences as gifts because they often masquerade as hardships, losses, illnesses, and setbacks. Most of us learn exponentially more through our hardships than we ever learn through our successes. These lessons are often the firestorms in our life, and they burn into us what we may become: brilliant beings of light and love. We also learn from family, friends, acquaintances, and even strangers like Damian and the woman in the taxi, who have confronted death, illness, bankruptcy, loss of home, or loss of family with grace, strength, courage, resolve, and stalwart love of life. They become our teachers. Without awareness and gratitude for these gifts, we miss the richness of life.

We have the opportunity to treasure the here and now, appreciate and contribute to every moment we're given, love openly and freely without boundaries, and welcome the lessons that undoubtedly come our way. Damian renewed this perspective with his recounting of his experience and the compassion with which he interpreted it. His story raised the harsh realization that money, greed, and arguments over earthly treasures such as inheritances have the ability to tear the fabric of our lives apart if we allow them to do so. When we choose gratitude for the people, events, and circumstances, good as well as challenging, in our lives, we can actually attract the positive energy with which we embrace them. Every action we take causes another reaction; we get what we give. When we greet our experiences with thankfulness for the lessons we are learning, which is often very difficult to do, we create an exchange of energy that is positive despite the circumstances. Through gratitude for all our blessings, great and small, in our lives, we have the opportunity to open the gateway toward individual and collective alignment.

Being Present in the Moment:
Moving Toward Alignment

Questions to consider:

- How might Damian's empathy for the woman he drove to Louisiana become a gift of learning for him? For you?
- Can you recall a time when you anonymously gave a gift to someone? What did that giving energy produce?
- For what are you most grateful? How does this gratitude manifest in your daily choices?

> *If the only prayer you said in your whole life was*
> *"Thank You," that would suffice.*
> **—Meister Eckhart**

Being ^{Present} Moment:
Moving Toward Alignment

Is this all there is?" Perhaps that is a question that has risen
in your mind at one point or another. It did in mine. This
question would invariably return at midnight when I was landing
in Frankfort or when I was in route to catch a 5:00 a.m. flight
to Detroit.

I was not afraid of long hours, hard work, or steep challenges.
In fact, while running on the corporate hamster wheel, I was
accustomed to spending long hours structuring, analyzing,
negotiating, motivating, and leading teams and organizations
through high-growth cycles. For many years, I loved it. I was
energized and thrived on tremendous learning experiences. At
one point a few decades ago, the questions changed from "what"
am I doing to "why" am I doing this? Why am I running so fast?
Where am I going? Where do I want to go? More importantly,
what contribution do I want to make with my life? I was grounded
in a faith and belief that I was created uniquely and for a divine
purpose, yet I struggled with "what that was" and how my gifts
and talents could be best used to contribute and serve others.

My corporate work took me all over the world—from Nairobi to Stockholm through New Delhi to Bentonville, Arkansas. My travels were peppered with incidental meetings with individuals and often strangers who unknowingly impacted my life. Over the years, these serendipitous exchanges made imprints on my mind and heart and served as catalysts for my ongoing growth and development.

Life is made up of thousands of these incidental interactions. We are all part of an integral and collective experience in life. Life is meant to be shared; relationships are the marrow of life. My intention in *Is This Seat Taken?* was to share a few of these incidental interactions and how these individuals offered insights that serve as guideposts along my personal road to alignment. They teach without deliberate intention. They teach through their simple actions, behaviors, and authentic presence. They are the anonymous sages who shed light along my quest to an aligned life.

From another perspective, we never know when we touch another person's life in that same manner. The conversation we strike up with the luggage handler at the airport, the interest we show in our postman's life, or the compassion with which we listen to a stranger's story in a hospital waiting room—all have more lasting effect than we may ever recognize. We all share the same ability to give love and attention to one another. We have the capacity to listen, support, see, and appreciate others, our coworkers, parents of our children's friends, or strangers in airport terminals. Yet only by staying present to those individuals who cross our paths will we be given the gift of their story.

Questions like "What is my purpose?" "What contribution do I want to make?" and "How can I make a difference in the world?" can upset a seemingly stable lifestyle. Through the inevitable shifts in life and ongoing self-awareness, our answers to these questions may also vary and change in priority. Often these incidental meetings and strangers come into our lives to give unexpected fortitude, perspective, and even wisdom just when needed most, if we are just awake, aware, and open to new insights.

There may be some reading this book who are running so hard and fast they may lift their heads and wonder, "Am I making the difference I want to make in the world?" In my work I hear many ask: "How can I continue to thrive when my choices are often in direct conflict with the current of the world?" "How can I stay centered and aligned to my true talents and beliefs when the pressures in today's arena push and pull on the very fabric of my being?" "How can I stay aligned to my desire to contribute to a greater good when the world defines success by material possession and hierarchical position?" I believe the answers are within us, are fueled through a divine power, and are often revealed and amplified through our unexpected interactions with others. We are often blind and deaf to these incidental meetings because we are busy frenetically catching a flight, closing a deal, managing a team of employees, or just dealing with the day-to-day pressures of living.

I believe when we stay present in the moment and listen to the whispers offered to us through unexpected sources, we invite greater awareness and can appreciate the gift of "a peace that passes all understanding," which manifests when we align with our true purpose. Through being fully awake and present, we discover our ability to become fully aligned to this purpose.

Thousands of individuals unknowingly contribute to the creation of our lives. We are living an ongoing journey. If we can turn off the competing distractions for just one moment and listen to the whispers being offered, what might be revealed to us?

My intention and prayer is that our individual and collective journeys are elevated by being present and appreciating each and every individual moment—whether they are joyous or difficult or sad. Each is teaching us something. I hope through our experiences how we may purposely contribute to humanity will be revealed and the "why we are here?" question is answered for each of us.

Readings for
Further Consideration

Bodian, Stephan. *Wake Up Now*, New York: McGraw Hill, 2008.

Braham, Barbara. *Finding Your Purpose*. Boston: Course Technology, 2003.

Campbell, Joseph. *The Hero's Journey.* Novato, CA: New World Library, 2003.

Chodron, Pema. *Start Where you Are.* Boston: Shambhala, 1994.

Frankl, Victor. *Man's Search for Meaning.* Boston: Beacon, 2000.

Hanh, Thich Nhat. *The Miracle of Mindfulness.* Boston: Beacon, 1975.

Holden, Daniel. *Lost Between Lives.* West Harford, CT: WingFire, 2004.

Jung, Carl. *The Undiscovered Self.* New York: First Signet, 2006.

Kubler-Ross, Elisabeth. *Life Lessons.* New York: Touchstone, 2000.

The Ryrie Study Bible, King James Version. Chicago: Moody, 1978.

Tolle, Eckhart. *The Power of Now.* Novato, CA: New World Library, 1999.

Warren, Rick. *The Purpose Driven Life.* Grand Rapids, MI: Zondervan, 2002.

Wilbur, Ken. *The Essential Ken Wilbur.* Boston: Shambhala, 2008.

About the Author

Kristin S. Kaufman is the founder of Alignment, Inc., formed in 2007 to serve individuals, corporations, boards of directors, and nonprofits in finding alignment within themselves and their organizations. Alignment, Inc. is a unique services organization that works with companies and individuals to create sustainable success individually and collectively. Kaufman has brought this expertise to hundreds of people since establishing Alignment.

During her twenty-five years of corporate experience, she has held executive positions at Hewlett-Packard, Vignette Corporation, and United Health Group. In 2009 Kaufman pursued and was awarded the distinction of professional certified coach from the International Coaching Federation and also achieved the designation of certified leadership coach through the esteemed program of Georgetown University.